CONTENTS

CORE SKILLS

Communication

FOR
Enterprise
GNVQs

Business THE LIBRARY
Management Studies
Retail & Distributive Services
Information Technology

JOE HARKIN

Collins Educational
An Imprint of HarperCollinsPublishers

Published in 1996 by Collins Educational
An imprint of HarperCollins*Publishers*
77–85 Fulham Palace Road
Hammersmith
London
W6 8JB

ISBN 0 00 320008 6

Acknowledgements
The publishers would like to thank The Boots Company for all
their help in the research of this book.

Commissioning Editor Graham Bradbury
Project managed by Lesley Young
Design and typesetting by Derek Lee
Cover design by Derek Lee
Illustrated by Harry Venning
Printed and bound by Scotprint Ltd, Musselburgh

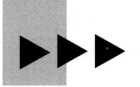

INTRODUCTION

This book is intended to develop the communication skills of learners taking GNVQs or NVQs in:

- Business
- Management Studies
- Retail & Distributive Services
- Information Technology

How to use this book

Step 1: select the LEVEL of communication you wish to achieve (LEVEL 2 or LEVEL 3 – if you are uncertain, consult a *tutor*) and study the *Communication Specifications* (pages 6–13) to understand clearly which skills you need to practice and improve.

Step 2: turn to the *Practice Activities* to practise these skills. If you need help, turn to the *Help Section* at the back of the book.

Step 3: when you are ready, complete *assignments* (following the suggestions made in the *Evidence Opportunities* section and/or set on your GNVQ course) to produce evidence of achievement.

If you wish to be assessed, you should consult a tutor before or during the assignment work and read the complete Evidence Indicators given to you on your GNVQ course.

Step 4: once you have successfully completed an assignment, record your achievement using the tick-box system provided in the first section of this book, and on the forms provided on your GNVQ course.

Do you have a recognised learning difficulty?

If you have a difficulty (e.g. hearing, sight, speech, motor impairment) you may make use of any human, electronic or mechanical aids that you normally use when communicating. The National Council for Vocational Qualifications (NCVQ) states clearly that appropriate provision should be made for people who need to use:

- means of communication other than speech, including computers, technological aids, signing, symbols or lip reading;
- non-sighted methods of reading, such as Braille, or non-visual or non-aural ways of acquiring information;
- technological aids in practical and written work;
- aids of adapted equipment to allow access to practical activities.

If necessary, please consult your tutor in order to discuss your particular needs.

Suited to the audience and situation (PC2) at this level, the student should be able to vary and adapt contributions to take account of the audience, situation and purpose of the discussion and her/his role in it (e.g. deliberately using a variety of language to help others understand the points they are making; expressing points/ideas in different ways to assist others; using specialist vocabulary accurately; saying things clearly; contributing at appropriate points; taking account of the formality involved; using suitable tone, manner and gestures).

Confirm (PC3) actively checking understanding of key points to show that they have listened carefully and understood what has been said (e.g. asking questions to clarify points made by others, re-iterating accurately the pints made by others).

Take forward the discussion (PC4) making contributions which build on the contributions of others and move the discussion on purposefully (e.g. asking follow-up questions, synthesising and summarising points made by others).

People who know the student (PC2 range) examples include other students, teachers, work colleagues, supervisors.

Level 2 Specification

Here are the specifications for Communication at level 2. Please also consult the core skills specifications you will have been given as part of your GNVQ course, and consult the person(s) who will assess you.

Element 2.1:
Take part in discussions

PERFORMANCE CRITERIA

A student must:

PC1 make contributions which are relevant to the subject and purpose

PC2 make contributions in a way that is suited to the audience and situation

PC3 confirm that s/he has understood the contributions of others

PC4 make contributions which take forward the discussion

RANGE

Subject: straightforward

Purpose: to offer information, to obtain information, to exchange ideas

Audience: people familiar with the subject who know the student (A1), people familiar with the subject who do not know the student (A2)

Situation: one-to-one, group

Purpose (PC1) discussions in which the student has to give information to others, obtain information from others and exchange ideas. Discussions may allow students to demonstrate two or more of these purposes simultaneously (e.g. exchanging ideas with a graphic designer about how best to use colour and typeface to create a front cover for a promotional leaflet; presenting a care plan for a client and discussing the similarities and differences between the care plans for different client groups presented by other members of the group; getting information from a personnel manager about the process for recruiting trainee cashiers).

Straightforward (PC1 range) at this level, the student should be able to contribute to discussions on subjects which are routine and commonly occur in the settings in which s/he is working, using the appropriate vocabulary to convey information and ideas clearly. Examples of straightforward subjects include discussing the Health and Safety requirements which have to be observed in the workplace; discussing different methods used for testing and inspecting the quality of mass produced items leaving a production line.

People who do not know the student (PC2 range) examples include heads of department, students from different tutorial groups/courses or department, visitors, customers or clients

EVIDENCE INDICATORS

Tick and date the box(es) when you have achieved the following:

Subject+Audience	one-to-one discussions	group discussions
straightforward+A1 or A2	☐	☐
straightforward+A2	☐	☐

The four pieces of evidence should include:
• discussions with both audiences in range   A1 ☐   A2 ☐

Check text (PC2) involves making sure that it can be read easily and is complete (e.g. considering the clarity of handwriting, that all the details asked for have been included and, where IT is used, the spacing, typeface and type size are appropriate).

Purpose (PC4) written material produced for a purpose in the settings in which s/he is working (e.g. to give information, to obtain information, to express or find out opinions, to exchange ideas, to present an argument).

Straightforward (PC1 range) at this level, the student should be able to produce written materials on subjects which are routine and commonly occur in the settings in which s/he is working using the appropriate vocabulary to convey information and ideas clearly (e.g. schedules for other team members telling them about their responsibilities in a forthcoming event; a letter to a local business organisation requesting specific information about its activities).

People who know the student (PC4 range) examples include other students, teachers, work colleagues, supervisors.

Level 2 Specification

Element 2.2: Produce written material

PERFORMANCE CRITERIA

A student must:

PC1 include information which is accurate and relevant to the subject

PC2 check that text is legible and the meaning is clear, correcting it if necessary

PC3 follow appropriate standard conventions

PC4 present information in a format that suits the audience and purpose

PC5 use structure and style to emphasise meaning

RANGE

Subject: straightforward

Conventions: spelling, punctuation, grammar

Format: pre-set, outline

Audience: people familiar with the subject who know the student (A1), people familiar with subject who do not know the student (A2)

Standard conventions (PC3) spelling of words used regularly should be accurate (e.g. 'distillation', 'confidential', 'maintenance', 'aesthetic'). Dictionaries and spell-checkers can be used. Sentences should be complete, using a range of structures and appropriate punctuation (e.g. full stops, capital letters, commas, semi-colons, colons) in order to convey meaning clearly. Correct grammar should be used; for example, sentences with subject verb agreement (e.g. using was/were correctly), relative clauses (e.g. using that/which correctly).

Structure and style (PC5) at this level, the student should be able to adapt the structure and style used appropriate to purpose to help the reader identify the main points and ideas (e.g. using paragraphs, sentences, headings and highlighting and specialist vocabulary precisely).

Pre-set formats (PC4 range) require information to be entered in clearly prescribed places with restricted space (e.g. record and report cards, application forms).

Outline formats (PC4 range) include those which have conventions in terms of layout and those where the structure is determined by others (e.g. business letters, reports where the order and/or length is prescribed, minutes or notes of a meeting).

People who do not know the student (PC4 range) examples include heads of department, those from a different tutorial group or department, visitors, customers, clients.

EVIDENCE INDICATORS
Tick and date the box(es) when you have achieved the following:

Subject+Audience	pre-set formats	outline formats
straightforward+A1 or A2	☐	☐
straightforward+A2	☐	☐

The four pieces of evidence should include:
- both audiences in range   A1 ☐   A2 ☐
- at least one hand-written piece   ☐

Images (PC1, PC2 and PC3) examples include maps, charts, tables, diagrams, sketches, photographs. The images selected may be reproduced or, where appropriate, cut out and used. IT could be used when students are producing their own images.

Purpose (PC2) the student should be able to use images when illustrating points s/he is making, in writing or in discussion, to help others understand the points (e.g. use two pie charts when explaining changes in the numbers employed in different industrial sectors between 1960 and 1990; include a diagram in a report to show how a pressure valve will operate when in use).

Use images (PC2 and PC3) the student should be able to use images to support the written and spoken communication s/he undertakes in the other elements at this level.

People who know the student (PC2 range) examples include members of a tutorial group, work colleagues, teachers, supervisors.

People who do not know the student (PC2 range) examples include heads of department, students from different tutorial groups/courses or department, visitors, customers or clients.

Level 2 Specification

Element 2.3: Use images

PERFORMANCE CRITERIA

A student must:

PC1 select images which clearly illustrate the points being made

PC2 use images which are suited to the audience, situation and purpose

PC3 use images at appropriate times and places

RANGE

Images: taken from others' material, produced by the student

Points: on straightforward subjects

Audience: people familiar with the subject who know the student (A1); people familiar with the subject who do not know the student (A2)

Situation: in written material; in one-to-one discussions, in group discussions

---

EVIDENCE INDICATORS

Tick and date the box(es) when you have achieved the following:

Subject+Audience	one-to-one discussions	group discussions	written materials
straightforward+A1	☐	☐	☐
straightforward+A2	☐	☐	☐

The six pieces of evidence should include:
• images selected from others' material as well as produced by the student

Select materials (PC1) at this level, the student should identify potential materials which may contain the sort of information required and select those most appropriate for the purpose. Examples of materials include notices, letters, extracts from books or reports, newspaper or magazine articles, instruction leaflets, maps, charts, tables, diagrams, sketches, photographs.

Sources of reference (PC3) examples include using dictionaries to find meanings of words, using operating manuals to find out instructions, asking a work colleague for clarification.

Level 2 Specification

Element 2.4: Read and respond to written materials

PERFORMANCE CRITERIA

A student must:

PC1 select and read materials for a purpose

PC2 extract the necessary information for a purpose

PC3 use appropriate sources of reference to clarify understanding of the subject

PC4 summarise the information extracted

RANGE

Materials: text, text supported by images, images supported by text

Purpose: to obtain information

Sources of reference: provided for the student; written, oral

Subject: straightforward

Summarise information: in writing, orally

Summarise information (PC4) involves identifying the main points from the extracted material and presenting them in a concise form. Students should be able to present summaries orally (e.g. in a short verbal report) as well as in writing (e.g. in a set of clearly structured notes).

Straightforward (PC3 range) at this level, the student should be able to read and respond to a range of material containing information and ideas expressed using the vocabulary which is commonly used in the settings in which s/he is working (e.g. a newspaper article outlining local objections to a new housing development, an extract from a magazine article describing the work of an artist, an extract from a book describing changing trends in numbers employed in part-time and full-time jobs).

Purpose (PC1 and PC2) the student should obtain the necessary information from written materials (e.g. get instructions, directions, facts, opinions or ideas). The student should be able to identify and understand key points/ideas and extract the meaning accurately.

EVIDENCE INDICATORS

Tick and date the box(es) when you have achieved the following:

Subject	text	text supported by images	images supported by text
straightforward	☐	☐	☐
straightforward	☐	☐	☐

The six pieces of evidence should include:
- a record of the purpose for reading the material
- a statement of the oral and written sources of reference used to clarify understanding
- at least two oral and two written summaries of information extracted from the materials read

Suited to the audience and situation (PC2) at this level, the student should be able to vary and adapt contributions to take account of the audience, situation and purpose of the discussion and their role in it, choosing how and when to participate (e.g. using vocabulary precisely and organising contributions to match the demands of the situation; using a variety of language and suitable markers to help others understand the point the student is making; saying things clearly; contributing at appropriate points; taking account of the formality involved; using suitable tone, manner and gestures.

Confirm (PC3) actively checking understanding of key points to show that they have listened carefully and understood what has been said (e.g. asking questions to clarify points made by others, re-iterating accurately the points made by others).

Take forward the discussion (PC4) making contributions which build on the contributions of others' and move the discussion on purposefully (e.g. asking follow-up questions, synthesising and summarizing points made by others).

Create opportunities for others to contribute (PC5) examples include: inviting others to contribute; encouraging others known to have alternative vie/additional information to contribute; expressing views which provoke responses; encouraging others to develop points they have made or re-state them in different ways to help their own an other group members' understanding.

People who know the student (PC2 range) examples include other students, teachers, work colleagues, supervisors.

Level 3 Specification

Here are the specifications for Communication at level 3. Please also consult the core skills specifications you will have been given as part of your GNVQ course, and consult the person(s) who will assess you.

Element 3.1:
Take part in discussions

PERFORMANCE CRITERIA
A student must:

PC1 make contributions which are relevant to the subject and purpose

PC2 make contributions in a way that is suited to the audience and situation

PC3 confirm that s/he has understood the contributions of others

PC4 make contributions which take forward the discussion

PC5 create opportunities for others to contribute

RANGE
Subject: straightforward, complex

Purpose: to offer information, to obtain information, to exchange ideas

Audience: people familiar with the subject who know the student (A1), people familiar with the subject who do not know the student (A2); people not familiar with the subject who know the student (A3), people not familiar with the subject who do not know the student (A4)

Situation: one-to-one group

Purpose (PC1) discussions in which the student has to give information to others, obtain information from other people and exchange ideas. Discussion may allow students to demonstrate tow or more of these purposes simultaneously (e.g. giving information to customers about the range of sports facilities available in a leisure centre; exchanging information about the different ways local employers ask job applicants to present personal information; obtaining information from a local architect about how he tackled a design brief for new accommodation for a local surgery/GP practice).

Straightforward (PC1 range) at this level, the student should be able to contribute to discussions on subjects which are routine and commonly occur in the setting sin which s/he is working, using the appropriate vocabulary to convey information and ideas clearly. Examples of straightforward subjects include discussing with clients the packaging and labeling requirements for delicate mass produced items which will be transported in different ways; discussing with other team members the contingency arrangements which might be needed if bad weather affects a social event which cannot be rescheduled.

Complex (PC1 range) at this level, the student should also be able to deal with more complex subjects, for example complicated reasoning, sensitive issues or the interpretation of others' point of view. This will require careful choice of vocabulary and structuring of what is said. The student should use specialist terms appropriately and to vary the way s/he expresses things in order to help other people understand (e.g. reporting to other students about how the local forestry commission tries to balance environmental considerations with increasing demands from the public for access to beauty spots; finding out about different ways of alerting young people to the dangers of alcohol abuse from a counselor who deals with alcohol-related problems; exchanging ideas with an advertising executive about the design of a promotional campaign aimed at a particular market segment).

People who do not know the student (PC2 range) examples include heads of department, those from a different tutorial group or department, visitors, customers, clients.

EVIDENCE INDICATORS
Tick and date the box(es) when you have achieved the following:

Audience	one-to-one discussions	group discussions
A4	☐	☐
A4	☐	☐
	☐	☐
	☐	☐

The eight pieces of evidence should include:
- both straightforward and complex subjects
- discussions with all audiences in range   A1 ☐   A2 ☐   A3 ☐   A4 ☐

Check text (PC2) involves making sure that it can be read easily and is complete (e.g. considering the clarity of handwriting, that all the details asked for have been included and, where IT is used, the spacing, typeface and type size are appropriate).

Standard conventions (PC3) spelling of words used regularly in the settings in which s/he is working should be accurate (e.g. 'psychological', 'confidentiality', 'representation'). Dictionaries and spell-checkers can be used. Sentences should be complete, using a range of structures and appropriate punctuation (e.g. capital letters, full stops, apostrophes, inverted commas, brackets, hyphens) in order to convey meaning clearly. Correct grammar should be used; for example, sentences with subject verb agreement (using was/were correctly), relative clauses (using that/which correctly).

Pre-set formats (PC4 range) include those requiring information to be entered in clearly prescribed places with restricted space, for example application forms, record and report cards.

Outline formats (PC4 range) include those which have conventions in terms of layout and those where the structure is determined by others (e.g. business letters, reports where the order and/or length is prescribed, minutes or notes of a meeting).

Freely structured formats (PC4 range) are those where the student determines how to organise and present written material appropriate for the purpose and audience (e.g. a brochure to encourage healthy eating by elderly people, a report for a marketing manager describing the performance of a leisure facility which includes recommendations on how to improve take-up by local teenagers).

People who know the student (PC4 range) examples include other students, teachers, work colleagues, supervisors.

Level 3 Specification

Element 3.2: Produce written material

PERFORMANCE CRITERIA

A student must:

PC1 include information which is accurate and relevant to the subject

PC2 check that text is legible and the meaning is clear, correcting it if necessary

PC3 follow appropriate standard conventions

PC4 present information in a format that suits the audience and purpose

PC5 use structure and style to emphasise meaning

RANGE

Subject: straightforward, complex

Conventions: spelling, punctuation, grammar

Format: pre-set, outline, freely structured

Audience: people familiar with the subject who know the student (A1), people familiar with the subject who do not know the student (A2); people unfamiliar with the subject who know the student (A3), people unfamiliar with the subject who do not know the student (A4)

Purpose (PC4) written material produced for a purpose in the settings in which s/he is working (e.g. to give information, to obtain information, to express or find out opinions, to exchange ideas, to present an argument).

Structure and style (PC5) at this level, students should produce material which requires varied choice of vocabulary and careful structuring of what is written to make the sequence of events and the main ideas coherent and clear to the reader (e.g. in terms of sentence structure, using paragraphs, headings, sub-headings, indentation and highlighting).

Straightforward (PC1 range) at this level, the student should be able to produce written materials on subjects which are routine and commonly occur in the settings in which s/he is working, using the appropriate vocabulary to convey information and ideas clearly. Examples of straightforward subjects include a set of instructions for others on how and when to use a particular first aid technique, a report which compares the performance of particular UK industrial sectors with those in other countries in the EU.

Complex (PC1 range) at this level, the student should also be able to deal with more complex subjects, for example complicated reasoning, sensitive issues or the interpretation of others' point of view. This will require careful use of specialist vocabulary and careful structuring of what is written in order to convey events and ideas clearly to the reader (e.g. a report of a site visit describing work in progress which analyses the courses and effects of delay in the availability of particular skilled labour, a report of an interview with a GP fund-holder which indicates the advantages and disadvantages the doctor believes the status gives her compared to the previous arrangements).

People who do not know the student (PC4 range) examples include heads of department, those from a different tutorial group or department, visitors, customers, clients.

EVIDENCE INDICATORS

Tick and date the box(es) when you have achieved the following:

pre-set formats	outline formats	freely-structured formats
☐	☐	☐
		☐
		☐
		☐
		☐

The six pieces of evidence should include:

- at least four pieces on complex subjects ☐ ☐ ☐ ☐
- all four audiences in range   A1 ☐   A2 ☐   A3 ☐   A4 ☐
- at least one hand-written piece ☐

Images (PC1, PC2 and PC3) examples include maps, charts, tables, diagrams, sketches, photographs. The images selected may be reproduced or, where appropriate, cut out and used. IT could be used when students are producing their own images.

Purpose (PC2) the student should be able to use images when illustrating points they are making, in writing or in discussion, to help others understand the points (e.g. using an organisation chart showing lines of responsibility for different care services within a local Health Authority when presenting findings of a project).

Level 3 Specification

Element 3.3: Use images

PERFORMANCE CRITERIA
A student must:

PC1 select images which clearly illustrate the points being made

PC2 use images which are suited to the audience, situation and purpose

PC3 use images at appropriate times and places

RANGE

Images: taken from others' material, produced by the student

Points: on straightforward subjects, on complex subjects

Audience: people familiar with the subject who know the student (A1), people familiar with the subject who do not know the student (A2); people not familiar with the subject who know the student (A3), people not familiar with the subject who do not know the student (A4)

Situation: in written material; in one-to-one discussions, in group discussions

Use images (PC2 and PC3) the student should be able to use images to support the written and spoken communication s/he undertakes in the other elements at this level.

People who know the student (PC2 range) examples include other students, teachers, work colleagues, supervisors.

People who do not know the student (PC2 range) examples include heads of department, students from different tutorial groups/courses or department, visitors, customers or clients.

EVIDENCE INDICATORS

Tick and date the box(es) when you have achieved the following:

Subject+Audience	one-to-one discussions	group discussions	written materials
complex+A4	☐	☐	☐
complex	☐	☐	☐
			☐
			☐

The eight pieces of evidence should include:
• all four audiences for written materials   A1 ☐   A2 ☐   A3 ☐   A4 ☐
• images selected from others' material as well as produced by the student

Select materials (PC1) at this level, the students is able to identify potential materials which may contain the sort of information most appropriate for the purpose (e.g. ensuring the materials contain all of the information necessary for the purpose in hand, are up-to-date if this affects relevance, are appropriate in terms of containing the fact and/or opinion required). This may involve using skills such as scanning to get an overview of the structure and content and skim-read to identify the main points. Examples of materials include notices, letters, extracts from books and reports, newspaper and magazine articles, instruction leaflets, maps, charts, tables, diagrams, sketches, photographs.

Purpose (PC1 and PC2) the student should be able to obtain the necessary information from written materials (e.g. get instructions, directions, facts, opinions or ideas). The student should be able to identify and understand key points/ideas and extract the meaning accurately.

Sources of reference (PC3) examples include using dictionaries to find meanings of words, asking a work colleague for clarification.

Level 3 Specification

Element 3.4: Read and respond to written materials

PERFORMANCE CRITERIA

A student must:

PC1 select and read materials for a purpose

PC2 extract the necessary information for a purpose

PC3 use appropriate sources of reference to clarify understanding of the subject

PC4 summarise the information extracted

RANGE

Materials: text, text supported by images, images supported by text

Purpose: to obtain information

Sources of reference: provided for the student, sought out by the student; written, oral

Subject: straightforward, complex

Summarise the information: in writing, orally

Summarise information (PC4) involves identifying the main points from the extracted material and presenting them in a concise form. Students should be able to present summaries orally (e.g. in a short verbal report) as well as in writing (e.g. in a set of clearly structured notes).

Straightforward (PC3 range) at this level, the student should be able to read and respond to material containing information and ideas expressed using the vocabulary which is commonly used in the settings in which s/he is working (e.g. a design brief for a fire resistant package, including drawings and descriptions of materials and processing required for a small batch production; a chapter describing the ways in which different management structures are typically found in different size businesses).

Complex (PC3 range) at this level, the student should be able to read and respond to materials which involve responding to more complex subjects, such as complicated lines of reasoning, sensitive issues or the interpretation of others; points of view. This may require an understanding of specialist vocabulary, the capacity to follow complex trains of thought and to form accurate judgments (e.g. a technical description in a journal of the development of a portable product for purifying large quantities of salt water rapidly; a brochure comparing the strengths and weaknesses of a range of graphics packages; a case history of an elderly patient who, despite increasing immobility, is supported by various local care services and, as a result, is able to continue living in her own home).

EVIDENCE INDICATORS

Tick and date the box(es) when you have achieved the following:

Subject	text	text supported by images	images supported by text
straightforward	☐	☐	☐
straightforward	☐	☐	☐
complex	☐	☐	☐
complex	☐	☐	☐

The twelve pieces of evidence should include:
• a record of the purpose for reading the material
• a statement of the oral and written sources of reference used to clarify understanding
• at least two oral and two written summaries of information on complex subjects extracted from the materials read

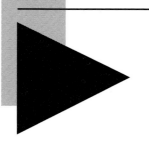

PRACTICE ACTIVITIES

The setting

Remedy is a successful limited company which manufactures and purchases a wide range of pharmaceutical, beauty and personal care, and baby products which it retails through a chain of high-street stores.

The company plays an active role in the community, primarily by creating employment and generating wealth, but also by supporting selected charitable schemes and by recycling waste materials from its manufacturing and retailing enterprises.

Staff attitudes are crucial

Remedy is a people-focused company which believes that satisfied customers are created by the attitude and behaviour of staff in selling good-quality, value-for-money products. The recruitment and training of staff are taken very seriously and each person is encouraged to work hard to achieve their potential.

The company believes that all people, both staff and customers, including the disabled, are entitled to be treated with dignity and respect. Staff are expected to display the right attitude to customers at all times – to be helpful and efficient because the customers are paying for goods and have the right to expect high standards of service; and to be cheerful and friendly to make customers' experience of shopping in Remedy as pleasant as possible. A happy, satisfied customer is seen as the best form of marketing.

Teamwork is essential, because meeting the needs of many hundreds of customers each day can be physically and emotionally demanding.

The practice activities that follow (pages 15–72) are based on the work of four members of staff in one Remedy store and the Managing Director of the Remedy group:

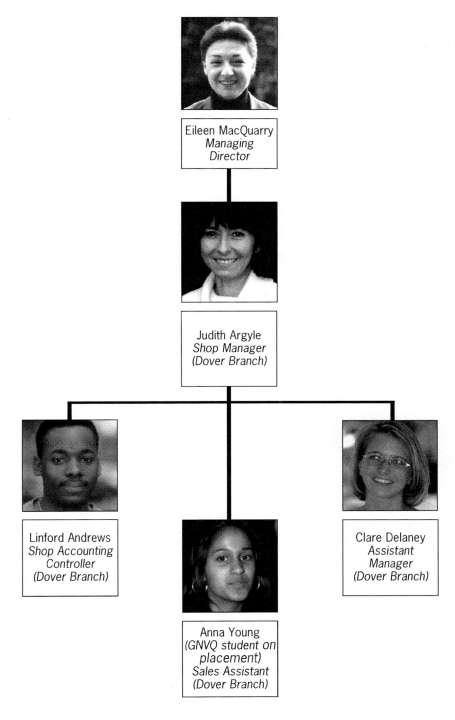

Eileen MacQuarry
*Managing
Director*

Judith Argyle
*Shop Manager
(Dover Branch)*

Linford Andrews
*Shop Accounting
Controller
(Dover Branch)*

Anna Young
*(GNVQ student on
placement)
Sales Assistant
(Dover Branch)*

Clare Delaney
*Assistant
Manager
(Dover Branch)*

In everyday life, people with different levels of skill and responsibility communicate with one another all the time. Clare and Anna communicate routinely in their day-to-day work at LEVEL 2 but also often communicate at LEVELS 1 and 3; while Judith and Linford communicate routinely at LEVEL 3 but also communicate at LEVELS 1 and 2 and sometimes at LEVEL 4. In these ways people communicate at many levels, adjusting their use of language to particular situations, so do not be afraid to use all parts of this book. For the purpose of gaining your GNVQ Communication unit, however, it is necessary to satisfy all the performance criteria for the level at which you are aiming.

1   Organising a work placement at Remedy

Anna Young is a student at a local college where she is studying for a GNVQ at Intermediate LEVEL. As part of her course, she wishes to spend three weeks in a placement at Remedy because she hopes to work for the company as a management trainee when she completes her GNVQ.

Anna knows that Remedy is very careful in its selection of staff and that even to be accepted on placement she will need to show that she can use a range of communication skills.

Introducing Anna Young

Anna can make contact with her local Remedy branch in three ways: by writing, by calling in or by telephoning. All three have advantages and disadvantages.

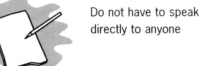

	Advantage	Disadvantage
Writing	Can make request plain	Do not know what information Remedy requires
	Do not have to speak directly to anyone	Writing is time consuming and there may not be a vacancy
Calling in	Remedy staff can see that I am suitable	The appropriate member of staff may not be available
	Remedy staff can ask questions as well as answer them	Time consuming / Nerve racking
Telephoning	Quick and efficient Remedy staff can ask questions as well as answer them	Nerve racking

Guidance

When gathering your thoughts about a decision to be made, it sometimes helps to write out a table or grid like the one shown here. Very often, you will already know the answer but need to see it in black and white to come to terms with it. Basically, Anna is nervous about using the telephone but knows that this is the best way to make preliminary contact.

Anna decided that the most sensible way to approach Remedy, in the first instance, is to telephone. This is more nerve racking than writing but takes a fraction of the time and allows for a two-way exchange of information.

Anna made some notes for the telephone call to Remedy.

Guidance

When using the telephone, we do not have the usual range of clues to tell us how the other person is reacting to what we say. We can't see their eyes, their facial expressions or their body posture. In consequence, we sometimes feel uncertain and even nervous. To help to overcome this, prepare to use the telephone by making notes; try to relax and talk in a normal voice, at a normal pace.

> Talk to the right person – Wish to enquire about a work placement – can you please put me through to the right person?
>
> Introduce myself: Anna Young, Drucker College. Taking GNVQ LEVEL 2.
>
> Work experience placement for three weeks – give dates. Wish to work for Remedy eventually.
>
> Ask question – Do you think that a placement with you may be possible?

PRACTICE

Guidance

If it is necessary to scribble notes during a call, redraft these immediately afterwards while the information is fresh in your mind. This is especially important if you need to leave a message for another person.

USE any opportunities that present themselves to make and receive telephone calls. Make brief preliminary notes of what you intend to say when making a call; and then make accurate notes of what has been said during the call.

Remember that to fulfil the Performance Criteria for TAKE PART IN DISCUSSIONS:

- what you say should be relevant;
- the tone and manner in which you speak should be appropriate for the subject and the person you are speaking to;
- you should listen carefully to what the other person has to say, and ask questions to clarify anything you have not understood;
- you should respond to what the other person says in order to take the discussion forward.

HELP
If you need more help in using the telephone, turn to page 92.

EVIDENCE

Assignment 4 (page 75) provides an opportunity to produce evidence of attainment in using the telephone.

Introducing Judith Argyle

Anna's call was taken by Judith Argyle, an experienced Shop Manager, who knows that it is important to put telephone callers at their ease. Judith started work with Remedy as a Sales Assistant and has been trained and promoted, first to Senior Assistant, then to Assistant Manager and then to her present job. She hopes to go further, possibly to become an Area Sales and Marketing Manager. Judith's communication skills are expected to be at LEVEL 3.

The **Key Responsibilities** of a **Shop Manager** are to:

- maximise sales;
- minimise stock loss;
- train, develop and motivate staff to deliver the required standard of customer service.

Above her desk, Judith has hung a motto: 'Effective management is achieving results through people'.

Answering Anna Young's call

Judith is polite and listens carefully to Anna, making a note of her name and the reason for her call. She advises Anna that Remedy does occasionally take students on placement but only if they show the sorts of qualities that the company looks for when recruiting staff. Judith suggested that Anna should send a brief CV, including the name of a current teacher willing to give a reference, together with a letter in her own handwriting. She might then be invited for interview, but Judith pointed out that this is not certain as the company receives many similar requests.

Anna thanked Judith for her time and help and put down the phone feeling disappointed. She had hoped to be told: 'Yes, fantastic, when can you start work?', although she knew that this was unrealistic. She would have to spend time carefully writing a CV and letter if she wished to have any chance of the placement she wanted.

The curriculum vitae (CV)

Guidance

All writers need to draft and rewrite, especially if the subject is complex or if the audience knows little or nothing about the subject. Redrafting is not a sign of poor ability as a writer – it is often quite the reverse.

Anna prepared the following CV:

Anna Young
40 Old Farm Road, Dover DO6 6BS
Tel: 01632 487978
AGE: 17

Qualifications
Dearing High School
GCSEs:
English	B
Maths	D
History	C
French	D
Art	C

Drucker College
I am currently taking a GNVQ Intermediate qualification, which includes the study of business management, customer service, information technology and communication. I have some experience of helping to run a College shop. As part of the course I wish to work in a business environment for three weeks, to gain as much relevant experience as possible.

Interests
I like music (I play the guitar); dancing; cinema; and travel.

Referees
Mr George Lake, GNVQ Course Manager, Drucker College, Christmas Avenue, Dover DO2 1BM Tel: 01632 778907
Mrs M. Fraser, 38 Old Farm Road, Dover DO6 6BS
Tel: 01632 286540 (Mrs Fraser has known me since I was 6)

The CV that you see here was not produced at one attempt. Anna spent some hours working on it. She drafted a first attempt on a word processor and showed it to her mother who made some suggestions. Anna then rewrote the CV and showed it to Mr Lake, her GNVQ tutor, to ask permission to use him as a referee and for his comments. He made some further suggestions which led Anna to draft the CV for the third and final time.

PRACTICE

Draw up your own curriculum vitae (CV). Show it to a tutor, relative or friend for comment and try to improve it, either in what you say or how you lay it out to create the best effect.

HELP
If you need help in using layout, turn to page 103. If you need help in writing a CV, turn to page 99.

EVIDENCE

Assignment 17 (page 77) provides an opportunity to produce evidence of achievement in using layout effectively. Assignment 29 (page 79) provides an opportunity to produce evidence of achievement in writing a CV.

The letter of application

Anna drafted the following letter to accompany her CV.

> Dear Mrs Argyle,
>
> I want to work in Remedy because I have often shopped there and usualy buy all my makeup there. It seems a very friendly shop. I am doing a GNVQ, as I stated in my CV, and as part of this I am supposed to have three weeks experience of work. I would prefer to spend this time in Remedy. I hope you have an opening.
>
> Yours faithfully,

Guidance

If you are asked to comment on someone's writing, try to do so in a positive and helpful way. We all need advice at some time and it is not helpful to be put down or laughed at.

What advice would you offer Anna about redrafting her letter?

Anna showed the letter to her mother who puzzled over it for a while. The letter did not seem quite right but Mrs Young could not at first put her finger on the problem; also, she did not want to criticise too much because Anna was trying hard.

Anna's mother tactfully suggested that Judith Argyle might be less impressed by where Anna does her shopping than by what skills she can offer. She thought the letter was a bit too short, giving the impression that Anna could not be bothered to write a fuller letter, stating more clearly why she wants the job. Mrs Young thought that the expression 'I am supposed to have' made it sound as if Anna is lukewarm about working at all. She noticed that the word 'usually' is misspelled and thought it a fatal mistake to allow any spelling errors in a job application. She also thought that the letter should state when Anna wanted the work experience. Finally, she asked if Anna was sure that it was 'Mrs' Argyle – is she married? Clare admitted that she did not know. Mrs Young suggested using 'Dear Judith Argyle' or 'Dear Ms Argyle', to be on the safe side.

PRACTICE

WORK with others on your GNVQ course to improve your writing by reading and commenting on one another's work.

HELP
If you need help in speaking and listening, turn to page 85.

EVIDENCE

Assignment 26 (page 79) provides an opportunity to produce evidence of achievement in reading and commenting on other people's writing.

Redrafting the letter

Guidance

This letter fulfils all the performance criteria for PRODUCE WRITTEN MATERIAL at LEVEL 2: the information is accurate and relevant (PC1); it is legible (PC2); it is written using standard conventions of spelling, punctuation and grammar (PC3); it is in standard letter format (PC4); and its structure (paragraphing) and style (vocabulary, sentence structure) emphasise meaning (PC5).

Using ideas of her own, and her mother's ideas, Anna rewrote the letter.

40 Old Farm Road,
Dover DO6 6BS
12 February 199_

Ms J. Argyle,
Remedy,
The High Street,
Drucker,
Dover DO1 2XZ

Dear Ms Argyle,

Following my recent telephone conversation with you, I am writing as you suggested to enquire if I may spend three weeks at Remedy (14 April – 5 May), to gain experience for my GNVQ Intermediate course.

The sorts of knowledge and skills that I think I can bring to Remedy are an awareness of customer needs, an ability to work well as part of a team, and a willingness to learn all I can. I am fully prepared to be a useful member of staff and will try not to take up too much staff time.

I am available for interview at any time and look forward to hearing from you.

Yours sincerely,

Anna showed the second draft of the letter to her mother and to Mr Lake, her GNVQ tutor, both of whom thought it was very suitable to accompany the CV.

PRACTICE

USE any opportunity that presents itself to write a tactful letter that you think is suitable in content and style.

HELP
If you need help in writing letters, turn to page 97.

EVIDENCE

Assignments 11 and 12 (page 76) provide an opportunity to produce evidence of achievement in writing letters.

2 The interview

Judith Argyle was impressed with the care that Anna had taken with her letter of application and CV and, as a result, Anna was invited to attend for interview.

Judith Argyle's preparation for the interview

The purpose of a recruitment interview is to select the best person for the job, based on the job description, and to present the right impression of the company to the candidate. Most large companies have clear guidelines as to the qualities they are looking for in applicants for particular jobs and although Anna is only applying for a work placement, if Remedy agrees to take her she will be treated as if she was a Sales Assistant on a training programme. Remedy has the following appraisal checklist for Sales Assistants and Judith read this to remind herself of the qualities sought.

Sales Assistant – Performance Assessment

1. *Sales and customer service*
    *   Generates ideas and demonstrates selling ability to enhance sales performance.
    *   Uses every opportunity to approach customers with a view to offering help and advice.
    *   Acknowledges presence of customers, recognises signals for help and responds promptly and politely.
    *   Listens carefully and responds with understanding to customer needs.
    *   Uses product knowledge and expertise fully and ensures that all opportunities for sales and additional sales are met.
    *   Takes responsibility to achieve individual and work group targets.

2. *Presentation*
    *   Presents a professional image to customers through own appearance and behaviour.

3. *Working with the team*
    *   Uses initiative and works with colleagues to ensure the smooth running of the store.
    *   Actively seeks opportunities to improve skills and knowledge and shares these with the team.

Like all newly appointed staff, Anna would not be expected to fulfil all of these performance statements but she would be expected to show the potential to do so after appropriate training.

From your reading of the **Sales Assistant – Performance Assessment** checklist, what qualities do you think that Judith Argyle will be looking for when interviewing Anna?

Writing summaries

As part of ELEMENT 4 (READ AND RESPOND TO WRITTEN MATERIALS) of communication, you must be able to write summaries of what you have read. Judith Argyle decided to make a brief summary of the **Performance Assessment** checklist, as a reminder of the qualities that a sales assistant should have. Here is her summary.

> SALES ASSISTANT
> ✗ takes initiative to get things done;
> ✗ good with customers: bright and cheerful;
> ✗ smart appearance;
> ✗ can work well with others.

▶ PRACTICE

USE any opportunity that presents itself to read and summarise written material by identifying the main points and presenting them in a concise form.

HELP
If you need help in making notes and summarising, turn to page 126.

EVIDENCE
Assignment 23 (page 78) provides an opportunity to produce evidence of achievement in reading and summarising material.

Anna's preparation for the interview

Guidance

The word 'businesslike' is placed in inverted commas to show that this is the actual word used by Mrs Young. The inverted commas also indicate that the exact meaning of the word may be debatable.

Anna consulted her own knowledge of Remedy, and that of other people (e.g. friends, tutors) to anticipate what sort of questions she might be asked and how she should dress for the interview. She decided to review her GNVQ notes on customer service and dealing with special needs; on the importance of teamwork; and on communication in organisations, including body language. She decided to dress smartly and to put her hair up because her mother advised that it made her look more 'businesslike'.

A friend who works for Remedy lent Anna a copy of a Remedy magazine in which she read the following:

Remedy's policy on charitable giving

Last year Remedy gave over £2.2 million to charity. Around 75 per cent of this was through direct donations; the remainder was distributed through Remedy Charitable Trust, an independent registered charity.

The company budget is used to finance donations where Remedy has a special interest and projects qualifying for support are sought on a proactive basis.

The company does not, therefore, respond to appeals, other than through Remedy Charitable Trust. The Trust's priorities are healthcare; economic development; education; family, maternity and child welfare.

Support for the community is central to Remedy philosophy. The company seeks to help in those areas where its shareholders, staff and customers live and work.

Like many other organisations, Remedy receives an increasing number of appeals for help. In 1980 the Trust received fewer than 500 appeals a year. Last year staff were approached with over 34,000 written and telephone appeals from local, regional and national charities.

Reading the article gave Anna a better idea of the sort of company she was seeking a work placement with and she felt better prepared to talk in

Guidance

Dictionaries are sometimes difficult to use because, for example, they give a number of alternative definitions. The correct meaning depends on context; that is, how the word is used in a particular sentence. If you can't work out the meaning from a dictionary plus context, ask someone for help.

general about Remedy. She did not understand one word – 'proactive' – and so tried to look it up in a dictionary where, to her confusion, the word did not appear. Instead, she read that pro- can mean a variety of things, such as, 'for', as in 'I'm pro nuclear disarmament'; or 'coming before in time' – as in prophet. This left Anna feeling even more uncertain about the meaning of 'proactive'.

Anna asked a friend who suggested that, in the sentence in which it is used, 'proactive' means that Remedy prefers to seek out projects to support, rather than reacting to requests. The friend gave another example to clarify the meaning – in a job advertisement you may read, 'Proactive person sought', which means someone who will take the initiative and not always wait to be told what to do.

▶ PRACTICE

WHEN you read letters or other documents that are unclear in their meaning, use appropriate sources of reference to clarify your understanding (READING: PC3). These may include dictionaries, encyclopedias, and consulting other people. For evidence purposes, remember to keep a record of what you clarified, and by what means.

HELP
If you need help in using sources to clarify meaning, turn to page 122.

E V I D E N C E
Assignment 24 (page 78) provides an opportunity to produce evidence of achievement in using sources of reference.

Interviewing technique

Guidance

Many conversations in life are made up of routine social chit-chat that makes people feel welcome and at ease. It is important to listen as well as to speak. Play your part in the conversation but allow the other people to have their say too. What is said is often less important that how it is said (i.e. whether the tone and manner are suitable).

Judith Argyle knows that people coming for interview are often nervous and need to be put at their ease. She greets them, introduces herself and gives them a few minutes to sit quietly before the interview. In this way the interview can get off to a more relaxed start.

Judith ensures that the seating arrangements are non-confrontational, to put interviewees at their ease and increase the likelihood of a positive exchange of views. When advising staff on how to conduct interviews, Judith expresses this by the following diagram.

Seating arrangements for interviews

non-confrontational   confrontational

PRACTICE

C ONSIDER whether you should use simple images to illustrate points.

 HELP
If you need help in using images, turn to page 116.

Guidance

Interviewing people is a LEVEL 3 skill, involving creating opportunities for the person interviewed to speak (TAKE PART IN DISCUSSIONS: PC5). A skilful interviewer should ask suitable closed and open questions that allow the interviewee to do most of the talking.

Guidance

In formal meetings, when some people may feel nervous, it is a good idea to find a way to let everyone say something in the opening minutes of the meeting. Shy or nervous people who say nothing will find it more and more difficult to speak as the meeting goes on. The responsibility for getting everyone to speak, without making a big issue of it, rests with the person who is chairing, or who has called, the meeting.

Guidance

You will notice that open questions, which allow people to talk freely, often begin with words such as, 'what', 'why' and 'how'.

Questions like these give Anna an opportunity to talk at some length, in ways that meet the Performance Criteria for TAKE PART IN DISCUSSIONS at LEVEL 2, and that give Judith Argyle enough information about Anna's personality and potential to make a decision. Anna's contributions should take the discussion forward and Judith's (at LEVEL 3) should create opportunities for Anna to contribute.

EVIDENCE
Assignment 18 (page 77) provides an opportunity to produce evidence of achievement in drawing a sketch.

The tone and manner (DISCUSSION: PC2) in which Anna Young will speak to Judith Argyle in an interview will differ to the way Anna would speak to a friend. She will probably:

● be more careful in her choice of words;
● pronounce her words more clearly;
● take turns to speak and to listen;
● use body language, e.g. the way she sits and maintains eye contact and verbal cues, such as saying, 'Mm, yes … I agree', to show that she is talking seriously and listening carefully (DISCUSSION: PC3).

She would also expect the Shop Manager's behaviour to be appropriate (e.g. welcoming, listening attentively, clarifying issues, thanking her for attending).

Anna may check her understanding of anything the Shop Manager says that she does not understand (DISCUSSION: PC3) by using phrases such as: 'Do you mean …'; 'I don't quite follow …'; 'Can I check that I've understood you …'.

At the end of the meeting, Anna might thank Judith Argyle for interviewing her.

The first questions that Judith asks are straightforward, factual questions that are not threatening – questions like, 'How do you like this sort of weather?' or 'How did you travel here?', allowing Anna to speak on a neutral topic. Judith can tell from Anna's answers how lively a person she is and may already have some idea of whether or not Anna is suited to working in Remedy.

Once Anna has spoken and been put at her ease, Judith can begin to ask more open questions that will give Anna a chance to talk about her suitability for the job. A question like, 'What do you hope to gain from working here?' is preferable to 'Do you hope to understand more about customer service by working here?', to which the only answer is 'Yes'. The first question allows Anna to express her own ideas and does not 'box her in'. Examples of other open questions are: 'Why do you wish to work in Remedy?'; 'How will the experience of working in Remedy improve your GNVQ coursework?'; 'What ideas and hopes do you have for your career?'

As a result of the interview, Judith telephoned Anna to tell her that Remedy was willing to take her on three weeks' GNVQ work placement in April.

PRACTICE

Make notes on how effectively you speak and listen to people in different situations. Pay special attention to talking to people with whom you do not come into frequent contact; and (for LEVEL 3) with people who may not know much about the subject you are discussing.

Make a few tape recordings of yourself talking and listening. You may do this collaboratively with a friend who is also interested in monitoring their speaking and listening skills.

How happy are you with your skills?

 HELP
If you need more help in speaking and listening, turn to page 85.

 EVIDENCE
Assignment 1 (page 75) provides an opportunity to perform this skill and to produce evidence of achievement in taking part in one-to-one discussions.

3 Anna Young's first day at Remedy

Introducing Linford Andrews

Guidance

Brackets, or parentheses, are used here to show that this is additional information.

Judith Argyle introduced Anna to the Assistant Manager, Clare Delaney, and to Linford Andrews, a trainee Shop Manager. Linford has a GNVQ 3 and, after some time spent as a Sales Assistant, he has been given responsibility (under the direction of Judith Argyle) of Shop Accounting Controller.

The **Key Responsibilities** of a **Shop Accounting Controller** are to:

- analyse business results and identify new business ideas and opportunities;
- generate open discussion with staff about business and individual performance and set clear, realistic and challenging targets;
- identify, with accuracy and self-confidence, the personal characteristics, competencies and latent abilities of staff in order to match them to job roles;
- motivate and persuade staff, to increase their morale and achieve targets;
- take action to enhance the skills and competencies of staff.

Linford Andrew's communication skills are expected to be at LEVEL 3. He is expected to employ a wide range of communication skills and to be particularly effective at speaking and listening because he is a key motivator of staff.

Linford was asked by Judith Argyle to look after Anna during her placement, to introduce her to other staff, and to offer her training in customer service which is the key to the success of the store. Linford greeted Anna warmly and said that he hoped she would enjoy her placement. He introduced her to other staff and decided to ask Clare Delaney, who had recently been promoted to Assistant Manager, to help Anna.

Introducing Clare Delaney

Clare Delaney started work at Remedy as a Sales Assistant straight from school, having performed disappointingly in her GCSEs. After a few years as a Sales Assistant, and after training, she has recently been promoted to Assistant Manager.

The **Key Responsibilities** of an **Assistant Manager** are to:

- fulfil all the performance criteria for Sales Assistants to a high standard (see **Sales Assistant – Performance Assessment** for Anna Young on page 21);

  in addition, fulfil supervisory duties:

- plan and organise staff to meet the team workload;
- train and motivate staff to achieve the required job performance.

Clare's communication skills are expected to be at LEVEL 2.

Writing a note

Linford Andrews decided that Clare would learn a lot in her new job by preparing some materials for Anna on successful customer care. Linford's first task was to motivate and persuade Clare to take part willingly in the training of Anna, and not to regard it as a chore.

From his own training, Linford remembered that there are different ways to get people to do things. He made a note of these, like this:

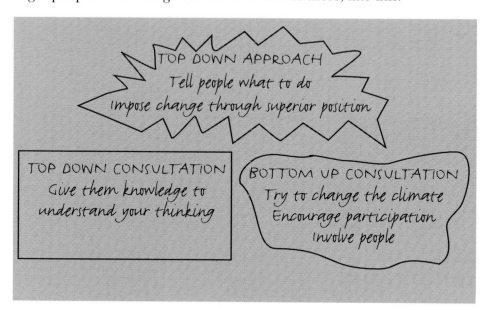

Guidance

In this paragraph, there are some words that you may need to clarify – coercion, morale and productivity. If this is so, then you could either ask someone who knows or use a dictionary. Never be afraid to ask.

He could simply say, 'Clare, I'd like you to produce some materials for Anna that show her how to deal with customers.' If Clare asked why, or said, 'I'm really busy, can't someone else do it?', Linford could use coercion by saying, 'I'm the Shop Accounting Controller, I'm telling you to do it; just get on with it.' Clare would have no alternative but to comply or possibly lose her job for not carrying out her responsibilities for training staff; she might produce the materials reluctantly; her morale may suffer, and her general level of productivity may fall.

Linford decided to take a friendlier, more democratic approach by saying, 'I want to discuss something with you, Clare. Anna Young is on three weeks' work placement. She needs to know about customer service. Do you think you can help?'

Guidance

Human behaviour is often reciprocal; that is, we react to people in the way that they act toward us – friendliness is likely to produce a friendly reaction; anger to produce anger, and so on. If you wish someone to behave responsibly, it helps to speak to them as if they are responsible adults.

Clare could say, 'No, I'm too busy'; in which case Linford could try to reason with her and, ultimately – if persuasion failed – could resort to coercion. In fact, Clare is more likely to say something like, 'What sort of help did you have in mind?' to which Linford could respond, 'She's only here for three weeks and there are other people too – weekend staff, for instance – who are not always available to attend training sessions. I think it would be a good idea to produce a handout on customer care that they can read in their own time. Do you think you could produce one?'

In this way, Clare is involved by Linford in the decision-making process. She may know that she doesn't really have a free choice – after all, the training of Sales Assistants is part of her job – but she may feel a lot better than if she had been ordered to produce a handout.

 PRACTICE

MAKE a recording (preferably on video) of routine conversations, both genuine and role play, with other people (friends, customers, tutors). Try to make these as natural as possible. What can you learn about your tone and manner in speaking and listening?

 HELP
If you need help in speaking to people, turn to page 85.

 EVIDENCE
Assignment 1 (page 75) provides an opportunity to provide evidence of achievement in taking part in one-to-one discussions with people.

4 Clare Delaney prepares a handout on customer care

Clare read the performance assessment criteria for Sales Assistants (page 21) to remind herself of what Remedy expects of them.

Taking ideas from her own training and experience, Clare drafted this handout for Anna's use:

CUSTOMER CARE

Remember that customers are people just like you; a friendly face and a smile are always welcome.

Be aware of customer needs – don't always wait for them to come to you – go to them.

Listen to what customers say and respond appropriately.

Get to know your products in order to give sound advice.

Take complaints seriously and **do** something positive to deal with the complaint and send the customer away satisfied.

REMEMBER that a happy customer will come back; you don't want a customer for a day but for a lifetime!

Use images: a sketch

Guidance

You do not need to be an artist to draw a sketch good enough to illustrate your work. Even matchstick people can be effective.

She drew a sketch to illustrate the handout.

Clare then showed the draft to Linford to see if it was the sort of handout that he had in mind.

Giving advice sensitively

Guidance

At LEVEL 3 it is important to be able to deal with sensitive issues which include the ability to offer sound criticism, tactfully expressed.

Linford read it and considered that it was rather brief and had missed important points that Anna should know about. However, he did not wish to hurt Clare's feelings (he realised that she had spent quite a lot of time thinking about what to write) and he liked some parts of the handout, including the sketch. He showed the draft to Judith Argyle and asked her opinion and she agreed that there were aspects of customer care, such as recognising the signs of someone needing help, and basic knowledge of the Trades Descriptions Act that should be mentioned. She also suggested that a question and answer format might be more user friendly. Judith advised Linford to use the sandwich technique of offering constructive criticism to Clare:

praise what is good;

tactfully criticise what is less good and offer positive suggestions;

praise what is good again and encourage the person to believe that they can do better.

With Judith's advice in mind, Linford spoke to Clare. It was a two-way conversation, in which Clare contributed ideas too, but here is a summary of the points that Linford made. He:

Praise
- thanked Clare for the draft, praising the layout and the sketch and some of the ideas. He suggested that the handout was taking shape but could possibly be improved;

suggestions
- suggested that more detail should be added about recognising customers' signals for help; the Trades Descriptions Act; dealing with customers' doubts; and closing a sale;
- suggested that the handout should take the form of questions and answers and added that perhaps Anna herself might come up with some ideas for questions;

Praise
- praised Clare for the time she had spent on the first draft; repeated

that some parts of it were very good, said that, 'With a bit more work, it will be very suitable'; and agreed a date by which Clare would have completed a second draft.

PRACTICE

OFFER advice to people in ways that are helpful, following the guidelines above. How well did you do? What can you learn about your tone and manner in speaking and listening?

HELP
If you need help in speaking to people, turn to page 85.

EVIDENCE

Assignment 6 (page 76) provides an opportunity to produce evidence of achievement in handling sensitive situations.

The redrafted handout

Clare made a second attempt at the handout, bearing in mind Linford's advice:

Guidance

A handout should be as brief as possible and should be set out in a way that makes the information very clear. Numbering and lettering may be used to emphasise meaning. Other devices include para-graphing, indenting, underlining, using bold, using italics, etc.

Guidance

This is a LEVEL 2 document. It is straightfor-ward in context (Clare is an Assistant Manager who should know about customer care), and it uses layout (in an outline suggested by Linford), structure and style in a way that enhances the intended audience's (Anna's) under-standing.

CUSTOMER CARE

Customers are people of all shapes, sizes, colours and ages who, fundamentally, are just like you – so a friendly face and a smile are always welcome

Question: How do you know if a customer needs help?

Answer: Use two of your senses: sight and sound. Customers may signal their need, e.g. by looking around for help; staring at the wording on packaging; or may even ask for help. Many people, however, will not ask for help, thinking that they would be a nuisance.

If in doubt, ask: 'Do you need any help?'

Question: What sort of help do customers want?

Answer: Advice about a product – so get to know your products well.

Reassurance about, e.g. a product's reliability; suitability for children; cost.

Question: What can I tell them?

Answer: The truth. It is against the provisions of the Trades Descriptions Act to make false claims about a product. It is also Remedy's company policy to offer sound and truthful advice at all times. It is better not to sell at all than to create a dissatisfied customer.

Question: What if the customer is still in doubt?

Answer: Draw the customer's attention to Remedy's policy that undamaged goods may be returned for a full refund on production of the receipt.

Draw the customer's attention to the Remedy's Fair Pricing policy: if the same goods could be purchased elsewhere at the same time for a lower price, Remedy will refund the difference.

> *Question:*   What should I do if a customer complains?
>
> *Answer:*   Take all complaints seriously.
>
> Do something positive to deal with the complaint.
>
> Refer the complaint to someone more senior if it is serious or if you have any doubt how to deal with it.
>
> REMEMBER that a happy customer will come back: Remedy wants loyal, satisfied customers who will return over a lifetime!

▶ **PRACTICE**

USE any opportunity that presents itself to write a handout or information sheet. Make sure that it satisfies the Performance Criteria for PRODUCE WRITTEN MATERIAL.

HELP
If you need help to produce written material, turn to page 95.

EVIDENCE
Assignment 13 (page 77) provides an opportunity to produce evidence of achievement in writing a handout

5   The staff training session on handling problem situations

Judith thought that more sensitive and rarely occurring issues, such as dealing with people suspected of shoplifting, should be dealt with in a staff training session run by Linford. A staff training session is a form of LEVEL 3 discussion – ideas are presented that are relevant to the topic (PC1) and clear to the audience (PC2); questions may be asked to clarify points that people make (PC3); by structuring the talk with time for questions (PC4), an opportunity is given for people to contribute (PC5).

Linford Andrews's first task is to gather his ideas into a coherent form for the presentation.

Guidance

When preparing for a presentation, it is often helpful to brainstorm ideas. As a first step in organising material for the talk, just write out ideas, no matter how unlikely some of them may seem,

PROBLEMS THAT COULD BE DEALT WITH

Dealing with complaints.

Speech that is difficult to understand (e.g. slurred, heavily accented).

Behaviour that is unusual (e.g. suspicious, boisterous, aggressive).

People with very wide pushchairs (for twins) or lots of baggage.

Small children with sticky fingers who are unsupervised by parents.

People who are ill.

People who persistently complain without reason.

People who have special needs (e.g. mobility, hearing impairment).

Guidance

Adequate preparation for a presentation is very important. This entails carrying out background research; judging the nature of the audience (e.g. size, attention span, age, previous knowledge, etc.); and planning the presentation.

Linford put the list aside for a couple of days but, during this time, he continued to think about it. One idea that struck him was that the term 'problem' is misleading because some 'problems' (e.g. aggressive behaviour) are 'owned' by the customer – it is their problem, although Remedy staff may have to deal with it; whereas other 'problems' (e.g. complaints) may be 'owned' by Remedy which, without knowing it, supplied faulty goods. Then again, other so-called 'problems' (e.g. hearing impairment, illness) are not problems in the same sense as aggression or shoplifting. In other words, Linford needed to sort his preliminary ideas into a more logical structure. He expressed these ideas in a chart:

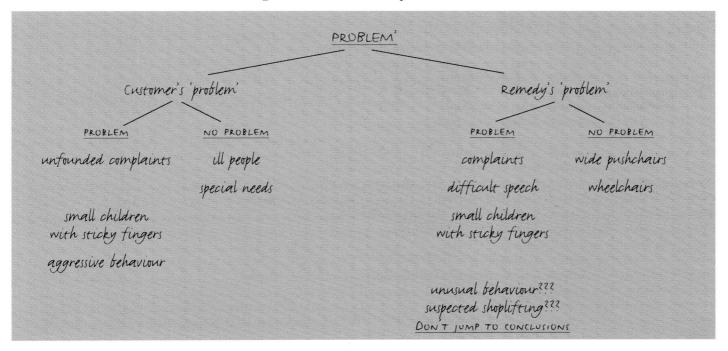

From his chart Linford could see that the store should welcome all people and offer access and adequate facilities for everyone. In the few instances where customers are a real 'problem', the situation should be dealt with in a professional way by well-trained staff.

Guidance

Once preliminary ideas have been mulled over, it is often a good idea to organise them into a more logical, coherent structure. Sometimes certain ideas have to be abandoned and new ideas introduced.

Use images: a sketch

Guidance

You do not need to be a skilled artist to produce simple images like cartoons. Even stick people can illustrate points very effectively. A little practice at drawing can produce some excellent results.

Linford decided to put his chart on to a large sheet of paper and he drew some simple sketches to illustrate each type of 'problem'. The sketches could be made into overhead transparencies to break up the talk; express ideas quite clearly; and act as a prompt for what he wishes to say. Here is one of his sketches.

Researching information

Guidance

Different libraries may use slightly different search systems. If in doubt, ask a librarian. Librarians are there to help people to get the most from libraries.

Linford thought it a good plan to give sales staff some more detailed instruction on handling customer complaints. He decided to consult a book about the psychology of customer care to get some ideas. He went to Drucker College library and searched the computer database, using keyword search. He typed in the word 'customer' and then added words like 'service', 'relations' and 'needs' until he came up with the titles of a number of possible books. He then scanned through the books to see if they contained relevant information and decided to skim through one book, *The Psychology of Customer Care* by James Lynch, in more detail. He came across the following table which he thought would be ideal to show to the sales staff.

	How to recover a poor customer care situation
Listen	Let customers get complaints off their chests, but do not tolerate personal abuse or bad language.
Apologise	Even if you are not at fault personally, apologise on behalf of the organisation.
Remedy	Take or promise some action to remedy the situation – use 'action words', such as 'I'll phone/contact/see so and so now/today/by such a time.'
Empathise	Show that you understand how the customer feels; why the complaint appears justified.
Redress	Provide some token, cup of tea, voucher, pen (symbolically flowers), use of 'private office', bathroom to help to make amends.
Follow-up	Check that promises made have been kept.

Source: *The Psychology of Customer Care* by James J. Lynch, Macmillan Press Ltd, 1992.

Guidance

If you do not understand something, often the quickest way to overcome the difficulty is to ask someone else for advice. Most people are very willing to help and sometimes, as in this example, it is part of their job.

Linford was not sure about the meaning of the words 'empathise' and 'symbolically' and decided to ask Judith Argyle. She explained that 'empathise' means to show that you would feel the same as the customer does if whatever the problem was had happened to you. She explained that 'symbolically' means that you show in a small way, by actually doing or giving something, that you take the complaint seriously and wish to compensate the customer.

 PRACTICE

WHEN you read books, articles and papers, check on the meanings of unfamiliar words and phrases. Try to identify the main points being made – sometimes it helps to summarise these in note form.

 HELP
If you need help in making notes from what you read, turn to page 126.

 EVIDENCE
Assignment 23 (page 78) provides an opportunity to produce evidence of achievement in reading and responding to materials. Assignment 24 (page 78) provides an opportunity to produce evidence of achievement in using appropriate sources of reference.

The training session

Guidance

This is a typical use of the word 'whom', rather than 'who'. 'Whom' follows a preposition – of – and refers to the object (Sales Assistants), rather than the subject (Linford) of the sentence.

Guidance

At LEVEL 2 in TAKE PART IN DISCUSSIONS, it is important that your contribution is relevant to the subject and suited to the audience; that you listen to other people and answer their questions, clarifying any difficulties in understanding. At LEVEL 3, in addition, you should create opportunities for others to contribute; for example, by inviting people to speak, or by remaining silent when appropriate.

Guidance

Making presentations is often nerve racking, even for experienced speakers, especially to people, like fellow students, whom you know well. Adequate preparation and a few simple breathing exercises are all it takes to overcome nerves.

Linford realised that he must bear in mind the audience – Sales Assistants – some of <u>whom</u> would already have quite a lot of experience of handling 'problem' customers, while others, like Anna, would be comparative novices. He decided, therefore, to create plenty of opportunities for people to contribute, whether to give the benefit of their experience or to ask questions and discuss issues.

Linford was slightly nervous when it came to giving the session. He knew that he had prepared thoroughly but, partly because he knew all the sales staff, he felt apprehensive. To overcome his nerves, he had a practice run-through the night before with a friend and, just before the presentation, he took a few deep breaths, dropped his shoulders, which he could feel tensing up, and relaxed his diaphragm. He smiled warmly and thanked everyone for attending and then began the presentation, knowing that he had done all the background work. Throughout the presentation he kept good eye contact with the audience and encouraged them to ask questions and discuss issues.

There is a tendency to run over time when presenting, so Linford put his watch on the table to check his timing.

 PRACTICE

EITHER alone, or with one or more people, give a talk or presentation on a topic of your choice. Prepare the talk with care so that the needs of the audience are considered. Try to follow all the Performance Criteria for TAKE PART IN DISCUSSIONS.

Use suitable images to illustrate the presentation and decide in advance how and when you will use them.

 HELP
If you need further help in making a presentation, turn to page 93.

 EVIDENCE
Assignment 3 (page 75) provides an opportunity to produce evidence of achievement in talking to a group of people.

6 Clare Delaney explains the EPoS system to Anna Young

Clare Delaney, the Assistant Manager, decided to help Anna to understand the organisation of Remedy. In particular, Anna wished to know about the interconnection between shops and how goods are ordered.

Clare sketched an organisation chart for Anna, which showed the flow of information.

HEAD OFFICE

Regional Office   Regional Distribution Centre

Store's central computer

Till Till Till Till Till Till

Each till has EPoS
(Electronic Point of Sale Scanning System)

> ### Guidance
>
> When explaining to someone how people and organisations interrelate, it is often helpful to draw a diagram or flow chart. This does not have to be completely accurate (that might be too complicated to be helpful), nor does it have to be beautifully drawn – a quick sketch may be enough.

Using the flow chart, Clare was able to explain to Anna how each till automatically sends data about stock levels and money transactions, via the shop's central computer, to regional office. There, staff can monitor each shop's performance and adjust marketing strategies accordingly. Similarly, electronic information received at the Regional Distribution Centre leads to the sending of replacement stock, adjusted in accordance with Regional Office's marketing plans. For special items, it is possible to make requests and enter data directly into the shop's central computer.

▶ **PRACTICE**

DESIGN a simple flow chart to show information. Remember the need of the audience to see the connections between different parts of the chart.

HELP
If you need help to use images, turn to page 116.

EVIDENCE
Assignment 19 (page 78) provides an opportunity to produce evidence of achievement in producing a flow chart.

> ### Guidance
>
> When searching for information, it is sometimes time saving and helpful to ask a more experienced person to recommend materials to read.

Clare decided to try to find some background information about EPoS for Anna. She asked Judith Argyle if she could recommend a book and Judith suggested that Clare should scan through some books available to staff. In one, *Consuming Passion* by Carl Gardner and Julie Shepperd, Clare came across information in a table that she thought would give Anna a much clearer idea of the advantages of EPoS than Clare could supply.

Guidance

A table such as this summarises information neatly. It is much easier to read than the same information expressed using full sentences in paragraphs.

Retail and distribution advantages of EPoS
Production of management reports
Overnight polling of data for head office

Stocks/distribution	Sales
distribution/route scheduling	more detailed receipts
warehouse/product location	product launches/promotions
generation of packing lists	shrinkage control
quicker stocktaking turnaround	brand data
unnecessary stocktaking reduced	quick identification of consumer preferences
correct goods to store at right time	more information for consumers stock control

Merchandise ordering
reports on invoices payable
automatic cheque writing for invoices
order preparation
eliminate unnecessary ordering

Source: *Retail Technology*, Euromonitor (1989)

 PRACTICE WHEN you wish to present information, seek out appropriate tables or images that will give the information more clearly than you would be able to do yourself.

 HELP
If you need help in using images, turn to page 116.

 EVIDENCE
Assignment 22 (page 78) provides an opportunity to produce evidence of achievement in selecting professionally produced images.

7 Anna Young works with all sorts of customers

Following her introductory training, Anna was given experience as a Sales Assistant. Remedy, you will recall, retails a wide range of pharmaceutical, beauty and personal care, and baby products. Sales staff are encouraged to specialise in one or two product lines in order to be able to give customers expert advice. Anna, who is only on three weeks' placement, will not have time to specialise, therefore, with her agreement, it was decided that she would spend some time on beauty and personal care products, and some time on the pharmacy counter. She was instructed to ask for assistance from one of the experienced sales assistants, or from Clare, Linford or Judith, if she encountered any 'difficult' customers.

Here is the opening sequence of a typical customer service encounter.

Anna: Hello, can I help you?

Customer: I'm looking for some perfume, but I'm not sure what to buy.

Anna: Do you have a price range in mind?

There then follows a discussion during which Anna lets the customer sample a number of perfumes, one of which is selected. The till transaction takes place and, finally, a closing sequence follows.

Anna: I think you've made a good choice.

Customer: I hope she'll like it. Thanks for your help.

Anna: No trouble. Goodbye.

Guidance

The effect of language does not depend on words alone but on the way that the words are expressed; for example, the word 'no' can mean anything from 'yes' to 'maybe' to 'absolutely not', depending on how it is said and what body language accompanies it.

Imagine these opening and closing sequences if Anna had a stony face or frowned at the customer throughout. The effect of her words might be reduced or even reversed. For the words to appear sincere, it is necessary that they are accompanied by appropriate non-verbal behaviour – for example, by a smile, eye contact, friendly tone of voice.

Most encounters with customers are of this sort: friendly, two-way and relaxed. In other words, they are the same sorts of communication as in the rest of daily life. Sometimes, an individual may not feel cheerful but will put on a smiling face because the wheels of life are oiled by human co-operation. People expect that communication with professionals, whether it is with a doctor, plumber or a sales assistant, will be fairly pleasant.

Occasionally, customers will be encountered who, for a variety of reasons, may pose extra challenges. Here are some examples which Anna encountered.

The return of 'faulty' goods

A woman came to the counter with a lipstick that she claimed was broken. She did not have a receipt. The lipstick case was scratched. Anna passed the complaint to a full-time assistant who looked at the lipstick and recognised it as a colour that had not been stocked for months. She explained to the woman that all lipsticks are checked before sale, that it must have been purchased months before, and that it looked as if it had been used. She returned it to the customer and said, 'I'm sorry, I'm afraid we can't change it.'

The customer became angry and demanded to see the manager. Clare Delaney came over and had the situation explained to her. She immediately asked the customer what shade of lipstick she would like and asked the Sales Assistant to put it through the till without charge. Clare apologised to the customer for any problems she had had, but without agreeing that the lipstick was faulty.

Later that day, Clare asked the Sales Assistant and Anna to have a word with her in private. She explained that it is not worth making a fuss over a lipstick, regardless of whether the claim is genuine or not. It is possible to take initiative to deal with little things as simply and quickly as possible. In a case like this, Clare advised, the customer should have been given a replacement immediately.

'But', Anna asked, 'what if she comes back again and again, whenever she is fed up with her lipstick?'

Guidance

Notice that Clare gives the advice privately to Anna and the Sales Assistant. This is less confrontational and more effective than criticising people in public. Dealing with complex, sensitive situations like this is part of LEVEL 3 skills.

Clare explained that that would be different and that then she, or someone more senior, would have to be consulted and they would probably refund or replace the goods but ask the woman not to use the shop in future.

The suspected shoplifter

Anna noticed that a customer was looking furtive and seemed to be placing goods in an inside pocket. She pointed this out to the Sales Assistant with whom she was working, who suggested that Anna should offer the customer a basket.

Anna took a basket to the customer and said, 'Would you like a basket for those goods?' The customer looked very surprised but thanked Anna. Some time later, Anna could see that the goods were in the basket and the customer was queuing at a till. The full-time Sales Assistant explained that most theft can be prevented if potential shoplifters know that staff are alert.

The customer who slurred his words

Anna was working on the pharmacy counter when a customer came in who appeared to be drunk. He slurred his words so that Anna could hardly understand what he was saying. She spoke quietly to Linford Andrews, who was also working on the counter at the time. Linford took over the transaction, listened to the customer in the normal, polite way and sold him the goods he requested. When the customer had gone, Linford explained to Anna that the man was not drunk but was a regular customer suffering the after effects of an illness which had impaired his speech. He pointed out that, on a pharmacy counter, it is particularly important not to jump to the wrong conclusions about customers' behaviour.

The child with sticky fingers

Anna was working on the pharmacy counter at a time when a woman with a toddler was waiting for a prescription. Unnoticed by the woman, the toddler had wandered over to a module wall display of brightly coloured baby clothes and was trying to remove garments.

Anna could see that the child was in danger of pulling down a whole rack of clothes so she ran over and spoke to the child. She took the child by the hand and led him back to the woman who looked as if she didn't know whether to shout at the child, shout at Anna or look sheepish. Anna calmed the situation by smiling and saying in a normal tone of voice: 'I noticed that he was about to get into a pickle.' The woman smiled too and apologised for letting the child wander away.

Guidance

Most awkward situations can be handled with a smile and a shrug. Think of people bumping into each other by accident in crowded streets – only someone looking for trouble would make a fuss – normally, both people will apologise quickly and carry on. Human life is made up of many such co-operative acts.

PRACTICE

MAKE a recording (preferably on video) of routine conversations, both genuine and in role play, with other people (friends, customers, tutors). Try to make these as natural as possible. What can you learn about your tone and manner in speaking and listening?

Imagine the sorts of embarrassing situations that could arise in a public situation with which you are familiar. How do you think they should be handled? Do you think you have the necessary skills to handle them effectively?

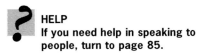

HELP
If you need help in speaking to people, turn to page 85.

EVIDENCE

Assignment 1 (page 75) provides an opportunity to provide evidence of achievement in taking part in one-to-one discussions with people.

8   The security memo

Infrequently, stores receive a memo from the Security Manager about customers who are a persistent nuisance. Here is a typical memo.

> **FOR THE ATTENTION OF:**
> **Store Manager**
> **Security Staff**
>
> SECURITY   *Suspicious Claims*
>
> Details are sought regarding incidents where small claims have been made by a woman claiming a product purchased had leaked on clothing or other purchases.
>
> UPDATE   Remedy has been subject to numerous small claims by a woman who alleged that products purchased in our stores had leaked on other goods or clothing. The woman was subsequently prosecuted.
>
> Recently, a woman of similar description visited the Remedy shop in Ashford and claimed that a bottle of toilet cleaner had leaked on clothing in her shopping bag. The clothing was a mix of male and female clothing of differing sizes. The woman gave her name as Mrs Paula Hatcher of 22 The Hill, Markshot, Surrey.
>
> She is described as about 25–30 years of age, approximately 1.7 m tall, slim build, blonde. She was wearing a long blue coat and knee-length boots.
>
> ACTION 1 Please brief store and security staff.
> 2 If a woman of similar description and using a similar story makes a claim, refer the matter to the store manager.
> 3 Pass details of any similar claims, together with names and addresses used, to the contact below.
>
> CONTACT   Bill Starwood, Security Manager: 01739 60241
>
> FILE   Action and destroy

Guidance

This is a typical company memo. It is structured clearly; is as brief as possible; and makes plain what action should be taken and by whom.

The memo format (a note to help the memory) states the subject as briefly as possible. It is not necessary to sign a memo. However, it should still meet all the Performance Criteria for PREPARE WRITTEN MATERIAL.

The memo was sent to Judith Argyle who put it on her agenda for the next meeting of sales staff.

 PRACTICE

USE any opportunity that presents itself to write a memo or note to somebody. Try to make it brief and clear.

 HELP
If you need help in writing memos, turn to page 97.

 EVIDENCE
Assignment 10 (page 76) provides an opportunity to provide evidence of achievement in writing a memo.

9 The paperwork of a sales meeting

Sales staff meet once a month to discuss any issues that individuals think are important.

The meetings are chaired by the Shop Manager, Judith Argyle, and one of the Sales Assistants acts as secretary by taking notes so that, following the meeting, minutes can be circulated. On this occasion, Anna Young was given the opportunity to act as secretary to the meeting, although Judith checked her draft minutes.

Judith Argyle circulated a notice in advance so that people could flag up any issues they wished to be discussed. Here is a typical notice:

The next monthly meeting of

sales staff will be held on

25 APRIL.

Please let me have any items for

the agenda by 18 April.

Once she has received the replies, the Shop Manager writes the agenda and circulates it in advance so that people can think about the issues.

<table>
<tr><td>

Guidance

This is a typical agenda structure for meetings in businesses, schools, colleges, and government departments. It deals logically with the business of the meeting.

</td></tr>
</table>

The next monthly meeting of sales staff will be held on 25 April in the Staff Room.

AGENDA

1. Apologies for absence
2. Minutes of the last meeting
3. Matters arising
4. Introducing OLAF
5. Reporting accidents
6. Security memo
7. Any other business
8. Date of next meeting

The minutes

After the meeting the person who took the notes (usually the secretary, but often another person, sometimes the chairperson) should write them up for circulation to all those who attended the meeting.

Here are the minutes of the meeting of sales staff, prepared by Anna Young and checked by Judith Argyle:

Minutes of the monthly meeting of sales staff held on 25 April in the Staff Room.

Present: Linford Andrews, Michelle Firth, Hasan Alman, Paul Gooding, Anna Young, Carl Russell, Helen O'Donnell, Clare Delaney, Mary Wong, Maria Dodds, Judith Argyle, Tanya Kumari, Emma Davidson.

1. **Apologies**: Kirsten Brenner, Liam Connolly, Steven Grant, Linda Hayes, Deepak Vora, Karen Humphries.
2. **Minutes of the last meeting**: the minutes of the last meeting were accepted as a true record.
3. **Matters arising**: there were no matters arising.
4. **Introducing OLAF**: Judith Argyle reported that OLAF (the On-Line Authorisation Facility) is now operational. All tills are connected to the Head Office central computer and via Barclay's computerised link to issuing banks for approval of debit and credit card transactions. The system takes less than eight seconds per transaction.
Use of OLAF will not affect the staff bonus of £50 for spotting fraudulent use of credit or debit cards.

Guidance

This is a typical set of minutes from a meeting. They should be as brief as possible, while still being accurate and representing fairly what has been discussed. It is particularly important that, if action is to be taken, it is clear what this will be and who will carry it out.

In some cases, for example with official company meetings, the minutes may act as a record of what was agreed, which may be used as evidence in a court of law. For this reason, they are usually presented to the next meeting for comment and approval as an accurate record.

5. **Accidents**: Linford Andrews, who is assisting the Manager as Health & Safety Officer for the store, requested that accidents, whether to customers or staff, be reported promptly. Linford will draw up guidelines and a form for staff use.

ACTION: **Linford Andrews**

6. **Security memo**: Judith Argyle drew staff's attention to a memo from the Security Manager re suspicious claims.

ACTION: **All sales staff to be aware**

7. **Any other business**: staff were reminded that they should wear name badges at all times while on duty.

8. **The next meeting will take place on 23 May**

These minutes are LEVEL 2 for PREPARE WRITTEN MATERIAL because they deal with routine matters and are written for people who will be familiar with the subject matter. However, some minutes may be at LEVEL 3 if they deal with complex and/or sensitive issues; or are written for people unfamiliar with the subject.

 PRACTICE

USE any opportunity that arises to write the minutes of a meeting. For example, you may attend a meeting and offer to take the minutes in order to gain practice. Take a look at the minutes of meetings (preferably of meetings you have attended). Are they accurate but brief? Do they make plain what action should be taken, and by whom?

 HELP
If you need more help in writing minutes of meetings, turn to page 101.

 EVIDENCE
Assignment 8 (page 76) provides an opportunity to produce evidence of achievement in writing the minutes of a meeting.

10 The report form

Following the sales staff meeting, Linford Andrews had to design a simple form for staff to use when reporting accidents. He wanted the form to be straightforward to use and to be easy to keep on file.

Filing Code _____

REMEDY

ACCIDENT REPORT FORM

Note: an accident is an event that results in loss or injury, e.g. a customer falls after slipping on a wet floor; a member of staff injures her back lifting goods.

Date and time of the accident:

Place of accident:

Name and job role of person reporting accident:

Please describe briefly what happened:

Give the names of injured people:

Briefly describe the injuries:

Were the following steps taken?

First Aid given   Yes/No

Who gave First Aid?

Was an ambulance called?   Yes/No

Time of call:

Time of arrival at store:

Signed _____   Date_____

TO BE COMPLETED BY THE HEALTH & SAFETY OFFICER:

What subsequent action was taken to prevent a recurrence?

What further steps should be taken to improve Health & Safety provision?

Signed _____   Date_____

 **PRACTICE**

ASK if you may study a copy of the standard accident report forms used at school/college/work. How well designed do you think they are? Do they cover all the information that is needed? Are they reasonably easy to use? Can they be filed so that they can be found again easily?

There may be an opportunity to redesign a form, or to design a new form that will help to record facts simply and clearly.

 HELP
If you need help in using layout when producing written material, turn to page 103.

 EVIDENCE
Assignment 17 (page 77) provides an opportunity to produce evidence of achievement in using layout effectively.

11 Judith Argyle handles a sensitive situation

On rare occasions it may be necessary for a manager to talk to a member of staff about very sensitive issues, such as disciplinary matters, appearance or personal hygiene. Topics such as these require delicacy and thoughtfulness if feelings are not to be hurt and relationships damaged.

Clare Delaney, the Assistant Manager, can't help noticing that a Sales Assistant has a problem with body odour. The person involved seems oblivious to this but other staff have passed remarks and Clare has also seen customers react. She feels that she should do something but does not know quite what to say. She decides that it would not be disloyal to her colleague to have a word with Judith Argyle, the Shop Manager. Judith is more experienced and, as the assistant is an older woman, Clare thinks the problem might best be dealt with by a more senior member of staff.

Judith decided to assess the problem for herself. She did not doubt what Clare said but needed to be sure that there really was a problem. There was. Judith then had to decide how to handle the situation sensitively. She knew that there were several ways to proceed, depending on the personalities involved, so the first thing to do was to decide on the best strategy, given the particular people and situation.

● straightforward assertiveness ('I think you may have a little problem … have you thought of using X?')
● or a more roundabout approach to the topic.

Judith knew that, whichever way she handled the situation, the discussion had to take place in private and to be confidential.

Judith Argyle decided to ask the Sales Assistant with the personal hygiene problem to work alongside her for a while in the stock room, checking stock levels and tidying up. As Judith expected, the work made them both rather hot and sticky. Under these circumstances, Judith remarked casually that she sometimes had a problem with sweating and noticed that the assistant did too. She asked the assistant what underarm deodorant she used. The assistant said that she rarely used deodorant. Judith said that

Guidance

Disloyalty – or the belief that someone has been disloyal – is a major source of communication breakdown. People expect to be able to trust their family, friends and colleagues. In this example, it is important that Clare speaks to Judith only if there is very good reason; and it is important that both Clare and Judith keep the issue as confidential as possible.

they both deserved a complimentary deodorant after their exertions in the stock room and said that they could each take a unit of Judith's favourite product. Judith presented it to the assistant: 'It's very effective. Why don't you try it? I find it helps me if I use it regularly.'

The assistant was pleased to be given the deodorant. She began to use it regularly. The problem with customers and other staff disappeared and the assistant was never aware that her personal hygiene had been doubted because Judith had handled the situation with great sensitivity.

 PRACTICE

IMAGINE the sorts of sensitive situations that could arise in a workplace with which you are familiar. How do you think they should be handled? Do you think you have the necessary skills to handle them effectively?

Reflect on any situation that you have experienced that was potentially embarrassing. How well was it handled by the people involved? It is impossible to predict when such a situation will arise but consider how you think you would feel and behave.

 HELP
If you need help in speaking to people, turn to page 85.

 EVIDENCE
Assignment 6 (page 76) provides an opportunity to produce evidence of achievement in handling sensitive situations.

12 The customer satisfaction survey

Judith Argyle, the Shop Manager, was asked by Eileen MacQuarry, the Managing Director of Remedy, to write parts of a Business Efficiency Report. The report will summarise the Dover shop's level of success and outline strategies to maintain and improve all aspects of performance. For all service industries one particularly important aspect of performance is customer satisfaction. This may be measured by levels of sales, because satisfied customers return, number of complaints recorded, etc.; but these measures may not provide any detailed information about how customers feel about the shop. So Judith decided to ask Clare Delaney, as Assistant Manager, to find out more about customer satisfaction with the shop. Judith thought that, as Anna Young was on work placement, it would be beneficial for the shop to use some of her time to carry out a customer survey and that the experience would be valuable for Anna as well.

The questionnaire

Clare drew up a simple checklist of questions for Anna to ask customers and showed it to her. Anna suggested a number of amendments. Here are the questions, with notes to show how they were changed after discussion between Clare and Anna and then, finally, with Judith Argyle.

Questions on Customer Satisfaction

Begin with questions to find out if the person is a regular customer.

1. I am carrying out a survey for the shop, Do you mind if I ask you a few questions?
2a. Are you a local person?
2b. Are you visiting the area?

Section One: Respondent details

Some personal details are needed to classify the customer.

3. Sex M/F
4. Can I ask how old you are?
   Age 15–25 25–35 35–50 50–65 65+
5. What is your postcode?

Postcodes can give a rough guide as to how far the customer has travelled and, sometimes, their likely social class and spending power.

6. Would you consider yourself as:
   White Afro-Car Asian Irish Euro Other
7. Can I ask if you are married or otherwise in a permanent relationship?
   Yes/No
8a. Do you have any children?
8b. Are they girls or boys and how old are they?

Children	M	F
	0–5	0–5
	5–10	5–10
	10–15	10–15
	15+	15+

Section Two: Customer satisfaction

Most answers can be recorded quickly.

9. How often do you shop in this Remedy store?
   1, 2, 3, 3+ times a month/week
10. For how long have you shopped here?
    Years: –1, 1, 2, 3, 3+
11. Do you like the shop more or less now than earlier?
    More/Less/Same

Important questions – take time to write down the customer's opinion.

12. May I ask you why?

13. How much do you like these features of the shop:
    a. Layout   V.Much Much Little Dislike
    b. Colour   V.Much Much Little Dislike
    c. Lighting V.Much Much Little Dislike
14. How happy are you with the standard of service from the staff?
    V.Happy Happy Quite Happy Unhappy
15. How could customer service be improved?

Don't forget to thank the customer.

Thank you for your help.

Guidance

The layout of the questions allows for ease of recording of customers' answers. Most answers may be circled, except the two most important questions (12 and 15) which have space to enter customers' replies.

 **P R A C T I C E**

THERE may be opportunities during your GNVQ course to design a questionnaire and, in doing so, to provide evidence for PRODUCE WRITTEN MATERIAL. The level that it satisfies will depend on how complex the topic is (and who it is written for). A questionnaire on a complex topic may be at LEVEL 3.

Alternatively, choose any topic you think may be interesting to investigate among your fellow learners (e.g. sports activities; tastes in music; career intentions; food likes and dislikes). Design a short questionnaire, taking time to choose its wording with care.

After the questionnaires have been answered and you have gathered the information from them, you may make a short presentation or write a short report on your findings, perhaps illustrated with appropriate images.

HELP
If you need help in designing a questionnaire, turn to page 102.

EVIDENCE

Assignment 31 (page 80) provides an opportunity to produce evidence of achievement in using a questionnaire.

The report

Anna carried out the survey of customers' opinions by asking the questions of 100 customers, selected at random. Then, working with Clare, she presented the results in a short report for Judith. Here are extracts from the report.

Use images: tables and charts

Guidance

The report is as brief as possible (it will be read by a busy manager and will contribute to a longer report) and uses tables and charts to illustrate points. The report is numbered so that readers may easily refer to particular sections.

The questions and the report are both LEVEL 3 documents. They use freely structured formats and deal with a complex, non-routine subject.

Section Two: Customer satisfaction

9.   How often do you shop here?   *Percentage*

Once a month	7
Twice a month	11
Three times a month	23
Once a week	28
Twice a week	24
Three times a week	5
More than three times a week	2

From this it may be seen that most customers use the store at least once a week. This may have implications for the frequency of changing displays, in order to maintain levels of customer interest in new lines; and for staff behaviour – many customers may expect to be recognised by staff or even addressed by name.

10.   For how long have you shopped here?

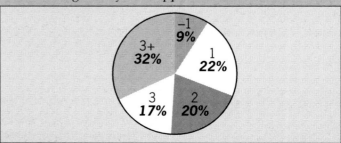

Length of time customers have used the store (in years)

From this it may be seen that, although the majority of customers have used the store for at least two years, a large number are relatively new customers. This may have implications for the marketing mix of goods, as many new customers are relatively young and may want new products and a different atmosphere in the store.

11. Do you like the shop more or less now than earlier?
     More 68 percent   Less 24 percent   Same 8 percent

Typical reasons for liking the shop more now were:

I think the staff are better trained and friendlier
The staff know about the products
The staff always have a smile
I like the colour schemes – they're varied and cheerful
The lighting's nice and bright

Typical reasons for liking the shop less now were:

The prices are much higher now
It takes too long to get served
You can't get advice when you need it
The displays change so often, I can never find what I want

From this it may be seen that staff attitudes are very important in building customer satisfaction. Levels of staffing, especially at busy times, may need to be looked at to ensure that customers get the speed of service they wish.

Guidance

When writing reports, it can be illuminating to give examples of what people have actually said, in their own words.

▶ **PRACTICE**

REPORT writing is a task that is often called for in industry, commerce and education. To become skilled at writing reports, you need to take any opportunity that your GNVQ course presents to practise this talent.

HELP
If you need help in writing reports, turn to page 98. If you need help in using charts and tables, turn to page 118.

EVIDENCE
Assignment 14 (page 77) provides an opportunity to produce evidence of achievement in writing a report.
Assignment 18 (page 77) provides an opportunity to produce evidence of achievement in presenting statistical information.

---

13 Linford Andrews's presentation about the Data Protection Act

Remedy keeps data about some customers' medical prescriptions on a system called Medihist. This information is covered by the Data Protection Act 1984. The Shop Manager, Judith Argyle, wishes to ensure that all Sales Assistants understand the legal requirements of the Act as they apply to them, and are able to deal appropriately with customer enquiries. She asked Linford Andrews, the Shop Accounting Controller, who is responsible for aspects of staff training, to produce some materials and run a training session.

Reading and summarising the Data Protection Act

Guidance

When reading materials, it is helpful to have a clear purpose in mind, possibly expressed in a few questions.

The guidelines to the act are 127 pages long, so the first thing that Linford had to do was to read them and summarise the parts he thought would be relevant for the training session for Sales Assistants.

Linford decided that he wanted to be able to answer two main questions:

1. What responsibilities do sales staff have?
2. What rights do customers have?

He also wanted to give examples of situations that might arise with customers so that staff would know how to behave.

Question 1: What responsibilities do staff have?

Linford decided to summarise parts of the Act. For example, the Fifth Principle of the Act is that **Personal data shall be accurate and, where necessary, kept up to date**. Thirteen paragraphs then describe the Principle. Linford summarised it as follows:

> Staff should ensure that all entries to the Medihist system are accurate. If in doubt, please check with the pharmacist or a manager.

Use images: a spidergram

To accompany this point, Linford drew a spidergram, like this:

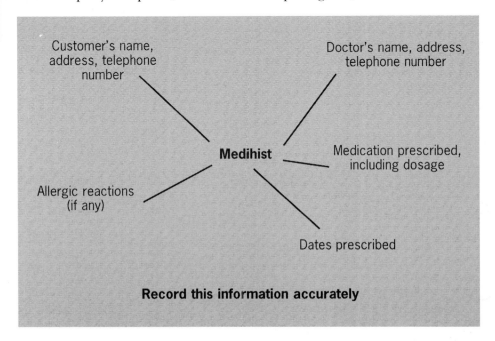

For some parts of the Act, Linford decided to use the exact words of the original. For example, he decided to quote the following criminal offence.

> An employee commits a criminal offence and may be prosecuted personally if he or she knowingly or recklessly:
>
> - uses the personal data held by his or her employer for a purpose not described in the register entry;
>
> - discloses the personal data to a person not described in the register entry.

Linford decided that the exact words would emphasise to staff that the information held about customers is strictly confidential and that breaking confidentiality is a serious matter.

Question 2: What rights do customers have?

The Data Protection Act gives people the right to access the data held about them. Linford noted, however, that exemptions may be made for health data. He consulted Judith Argyle who confirmed that all requests for data should be passed to her or the duty pharmacist, who, in turn, would consult the customer's doctor. Under no circumstances should staff simply give out information from the Medihist system. To illustrate the sorts of customer situations that may arise with Medihist, Linford drew up three example situations.

> **Situation 1:** The mother of a teenage girl wants to know if her daughter has been prescribed contraceptives. Should staff tell her?
>
> **Answer:** *No. The data of children is as protected as that of adults.*
>
> **Situation 2:** The son of an elderly woman comes in to obtain a repeat prescription. He brings a note from his mother. Should he be given the prescription?
>
> **Answer:** *Yes – so long as the note appears genuine and the repeat prescription is approved by the pharmacist.*
>
> **Situation 3:** The father of a small child, who is taking the child abroad, wishes to obtain details of a drug the child has been prescribed. Should he be given the information?
>
> **Answer:** *No. Once again, information about the child is confidential. The man should be advised to consult the child's doctor.*

PRACTICE

WHEN you research material for a presentation or a report, be prepared to search for relevant materials (PC1); study the contents and index pages for potentially relevant parts; scan and skim through material, searching for relevant passages; read these more slowly, making notes of the relevant information (PC2). If necessary, use appropriate sources of reference to clarify your understanding (PC3); and then, finally, summarise the material extracted (pc4).

HELP
If you need help to read effectively, turn to page 125.

EVIDENCE
Assignment 23 (page 78) provides an opportunity to produce evidence of achievement in reading to research a subject.

Making the presentation

Guidance

At LEVEL 2 it is important that your presentation is relevant to the subject and suited to the audience; that you listen to other people and answer their questions, clarifying any difficulties in understanding. At LEVEL 3, in addition, you should create opportunities for others to contribute, for example by inviting people to speak, or by remaining silent when appropriate.

During the staff training session, Linford Andrews will: try to keep to the subject of the Medihist system and the Data Protection Act (DISCUSSION PC1); fit what he says (e.g. in vocabulary, tone and manner) to the audience of Sales Assistants (PC2); check that he understands the points and questions that people make (PC3); keep the discussion moving forward (PC4); and make sure that everyone joins in the session (PC5).

PRACTICE

EITHER alone, or with one or more people, give a talk or presentation on a topic of your choice. Prepare the presentation with care and consider the needs of the audience. Try to follow all the performance criteria for TAKE PART IN DISCUSSIONS.

HELP
If you need help in speaking to groups of people, turn to page 93.

EVIDENCE
Assignment 3 (page 75) provides an opportunity to produce evidence of achievement in speaking to a group of people.

14 Staff sales performance

Clare Delaney's report

The use of electronic tills means that detailed information about the performance of each member of the sales staff is available. In preparation for the writing of the shop's Business Efficiency Report, Judith Argyle asked Clare Delaney, as Assistant Manager, for a breakdown of the performance of individual sales staff. Clare obtained the information from the shop's central computer and decided to set it out as a table. Here is an extract from the table, showing the average weekly performance of some full-time staff who sell beauty and personal care products.

Assistant	Transactions	Takings	ATVs *
Jane Osborne	121	310.97	2.57
Bill Tyson	230	887.80	3.86
Andrew Mace	193	808.67	4.19
Leila Patel	284	857.68	3.02

* ATVs = average transaction values

To accompany the table, Clare wrote a brief summary that included the following comments on the entries above:

- Jane Osborne is rather slow to react to customers' needs. She waits for other staff to help customers and makes little attempt to sell customers additional goods.
- Bill Tyson is responsible for more takings than any other member of the sales team. He has an above average ATV and is always willing to assist customers.
- Andrew Mace is very conscientious. The number of transactions he handles is below average but he spends a lot of time with customers and they often buy additional goods. As a result, his ATV is the highest of all assistants.
- Leila Patel is a good, all-round member of staff. She is very quick to help customers and also has achieved a relatively high ATV.

 PRACTICE

IT often helps to summarise information, using graphs, charts and tables, and briefly writing up the most important points. Use any opportunity that presents itself to summarise information.

 HELP
If you need help in using charts and tables, turn to page 118.

 EVIDENCE
Assignment 18 (page 77) provides an opportunity to produce evidence of achievement in presenting statistical information.

Judith Argyle acts on Clare Delaney's report

Guidance

When discussing a sensitive subject, it is wise to have any facts at your fingertips and to prepare what you wish to say. Remember that, in this situation, Judith's purpose is not to get angry with Jane (which may make the situation worse) but to get Jane to see that she ought to work harder.

When Judith Argyle read this account she concluded that one member of the sales staff, Jane Osborne, was not pulling her weight. To try to improve the situation, she decided to speak with Jane.

Judith reviewed the sales figures for beauty and personal care staff before seeing Jane Osborne privately. She asked Jane to have a seat and put her at her ease by making them both a cup of coffee and spending a few minutes chatting about general topics. In this way, Judith prepared for the subject of the discussion – Jane's poor performance as a salesperson – by avoiding any sense of confrontation. Then Judith introduced the main purpose. These are extracts from their conversation.

'I have asked to see you, Jane, because I have looked at the sales figures and you seem to be well behind other staff.' Judith showed Jane the figures. 'As you can see, you don't serve as many customers as other staff and when you do serve them you are not selling as much.'

Guidance

You will see that this situation is at LEVEL 3. It is a complex, sensitive situation. Judith needs to:

- make effective and relevant contributions (PC1);
- speak in a suitable tone and manner (PC2);
- listen attentively and respond appropriately (PC3);
- if necessary, ask questions to clarify what Jane Osborne is saying (PC4);
- encourage Jane to discuss the situation in a positive way (PC5).

Guidance

Notice that an apostrophe is used in you're, because it is short for 'you are'. The letter 'a' is missing and the apostrophe indicates this.

Jane looked rather embarrassed and did not know what to say.

Judith continued, 'Do you think that you are as quick as you ought to be to help customers?'

'Some people are quicker than me.'

'Would you agree that staff should share the load pretty evenly?'

Jane nodded but said, 'Sometimes I haven't felt very well.'

'If you are ill, that's a different matter. We can all have an off day, but these figures are for the whole year. Do you enjoy your work?'

'Sometimes. Sometimes it's a bit boring. Time can drag.'

'Do you think that if you become a bit more active in helping customers, time might pass more quickly?'

Jane nodded, 'Yes, maybe.'

'Let's see if, over the coming weeks, you can improve your sales performance. I want you to try to be more proactive in helping customers – don't wait for other people to take the initiative. All right?' Judith smiled.

'I'll do my best.' Jane smiled.

'Good. We'll meet again in a few weeks' time and have another chat to see how you're getting on.'

▶ **PRACTICE**

MAKE notes of how effectively you speak and listen to people in different situations. Pay special attention to conversing with people with whom you do not come into frequent contact; and with people who may not know much about the subject.

Imagine the sorts of sensitive situations that could arise in a workplace with which you are familiar. How do you think they should be handled? Do you think you have the necessary skills to handle them effectively?

? HELP
If you need help in speaking to people, turn to page 85.

EVIDENCE
Assignment 6 (page 76) provides an opportunity to produce evidence of achievement in handling sensitive situations.

15 The sales performance chart

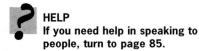

**Use images:
a pictogram**

From reading Clare Delaney's report, Judith also concluded that some staff may spend a bit too much time with customers – Andrew Mace has a high ATV but is not serving as many customers as Bill Tyson or Leila Patel and so his takings are lower. Judith decided to start an eye-catching, monthly position table for staff takings, to encourage people to increase sales by balancing time spent with individual customers against the needs of all customers.

For the four people in the table above, here is Judith's sales chart.

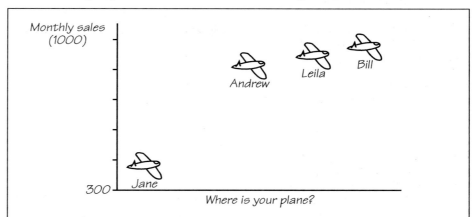

Guidance

This chart is an example of a pictogram, or a picture that represents information. A pictogram can be more eye-catching and fun to use than some other types of chart.

Judith agreed with the Managing Director, Eileen MacQuarry, to give Remedy gift vouchers to the highest-flying salesperson each month, and also to the person who makes the biggest increase in performance.

 PRACTICE

DESIGN a pictogram to record information. Try to make the chart eye-catching and clear.

 HELP
If you need help to use charts, turn to page 118.

 EVIDENCE
Assignment 18 (page 77) provides an opportunity to produce evidence of achievement in presenting information in a chart.

16 The Business Efficiency Report

If you look again at the key responsibilities of a Shop Manager (page 00) you will see that Judith Argyle is responsible for meeting the shop's sales targets by such means as organising staff and achieving the required standards of merchandising and sales promotion.

The part of the Business Efficiency Report that she will write has to do with these responsibilities. Judith gathers together the information she has requested from people like Linford Andrews and Clare Delaney and adds material of her own, gathered from computer data and from her personal experience of managing sales.

She gives her section of the report a title, Trading Information, and organises it into appropriate sections, for example:

1.1 Selling costs/Sales ratio
1.2 Sales staff recruitment and training

2.1 Sales/Stock ratio
2.2 Stock loss
2.3 Stock system changes

3.1 Boosting sales
3.2 Improving display
3.3 Improving lighting

4.1 Customer satisfaction

Each section will state the facts as clearly as possible (using appropriate images), emphasise highlights and include a short discussion of issues. For example, here is Section 1:

Guidance

The report should be as brief as possible and should meet the performance criteria for PRODUCE WRITTEN MATERIAL. It should include accurate and relevant information (PC1); be legible and clear in meaning (PC2); be written using standard conventions of spelling, punctuation and grammar (PC3); should be presented in a way that suits the purpose – in this case to show how efficiently the shop is trading – (PC4); and, finally, the structure and style should make the main ideas clear to the reader (PC5).

1.1   Selling costs/Sales ratio

The ratio this year is 26.4% (last year 27.8%; the year before 28.7%) indicating that, once again, the efficiency of sales has improved. This is due to a slight overall decrease in staffing levels, the use of more efficient staff rotas that cut down on overstaffing at quiet trading times, and better training of staff to maximise sales opportunities, especially in response to advertisements and other sales promotions.

1.2   Sales staff recruitment and training

SALES STAFF	full-time	% hours	part-time	% hours
Target No Year begin	16	73%	23	27%
Left	5		8	
Appointed	4		10	
Target No Year End	15	67%	25	33%

Table III

From Table III it may be seen that approximately one-third of the sales staff left during the year for a variety of reasons that included: pregnancy (3); other job (3); leaving area (3); ill health (2); dismissal (1), no reason given (1).

It was decided to appoint more part-time staff to increase the flexibility of staff rotas.

NVQ training has been introduced for all staff, linked to the appraisal scheme. Each member of staff is expected to keep a record of achievement and a portfolio of evidence as a means to enhance their knowledge of products and of customer service; and to act as a basis for staff development and promotion decisions.

 **PRACTICE**

USE any opportunity that arises to work on an extended piece of writing. It may be an essay, report or article for a paper. Bear in mind the needs of the audience. Ensure that you set out the information in a way that helps the reader to follow the line of argument or presentation of facts. Be prepared to make preliminary notes and to redraft and polish your writing to make it as informative and readable as possible. Consider whether you should use images to illustrate your writing.

 HELP
If you need help with any aspect of writing, turn to page 95.

 EVIDENCE
Assignment 14 (page 77) provides an opportunity to produce evidence of achievement in writing a report. Assignment 15 (page 77) provides an opportunity to produce evidence of achievement in writing an article.

17 Clare Delaney handles a customer complaint by telephone

Clare was asked by a Sales Assistant to speak on the telephone to a customer who was angry. Clare introduced herself and asked if she could help.

The caller said that staff at Remedy had been careless: 'I had some photos developed and when I got them home I discovered that they're not mine! What kind of careless bungling is that?'

Clare knew that it was very unlikely that Remedy staff could be at fault. Film for processing is put into an envelope with the customer present and then sent to an independent laboratory for processing. The processed prints or slides are then returned, ready packaged, for collection by the customer. If a mistake had been made, it was most likely to have been by the laboratory. The caller, however, could not be expected to know this and was in full flow: 'They were photos of a holiday and are irreplaceable. I want someone's head to roll for this. What are you going to do about it?'

Clare spoke calmly and asked the man for his name and telephone number. She then asked the customer, Mr Rogers, when he had brought in the film, what type it was, and to describe the photographs it contained. The caller explained that it was a 35mm film with photos of London sights, such as the Houses of Parliament and St Paul's. Clare made a careful note of all this information. She then asked Mr Rogers to describe the photographs he had received and was told that they were of a children's party. Clare made a note of this too.

Clare apologised to the caller for the mix up and told him that she would do her very best to discover the whereabouts of the missing photographs and ring him back; in the meantime, she explained, other people might be missing their child's party photos, so she asked Mr Rogers politely to look after them with care.

Following the call, Clare summarised her notes and then rang the photographic laboratory that processes films for Remedy. First of all, she introduced herself, then said briefly what the problem was and made sure that she was put through to a person who could help. Clare explained the problem and described the missing photographs. She asked that a search be made immediately for them. This was agreed and a promise was made to ring Clare back. Clare then asked a Sales Assistant to open every pack of photographs awaiting collection to check if they contained pictures of the Houses of Parliament.

Fortunately, the laboratory rang back within half an hour to say that they had found the missing prints and would have a courier bring them over straightaway.

Clare phoned the customer and explained that the laboratory had made a mix up – which was most unusual – but that the photographs had been found and would be ready for collection at any time. She apologised once again for the problem and said that Remedy would refund the cost of processing and give the customer a free film.

Guidance

Every complaint should be taken seriously but without jumping to conclusions. Most complaints can be dealt with by listening and responding sensitively, without need for time-consuming form filling, the involvement of other people, or argument. It is most important to carry out any promises made in order to resolve a complaint.

Guidance

The name of St Paul's has an apostrophe because, in a sense, the cathedral belongs to St Paul, so the apostrophe shows possession.

Guidance

If it is necessary to scribble notes during a call, redraft these straight afterwards while the information is fresh in your mind. This is especially important if you need to leave a message for another person.

 **PRACTICE**

USE any opportunities that present themselves to make and receive telephone calls. Make brief preliminary notes of what you intend to say when making a call; and make accurate notes of what has been said during a call.

Remember the Performance Criteria for TAKE PART IN DISCUSSIONS:

 HELP
If you need more help in using the telephone, turn to page 92.

 EVIDENCE
Assignment 4 (page 75) provides an opportunity to produce evidence of attainment in using the telephone.

18 Linford Andrews helps staff to use the telephone effectively

It was plain to Linford Andrews that some of the staff were nervous about making telephone calls. To help them he drew up a chart containing useful advice, basing this on an acronym (a word formed from the initial letters of other words) to help them to memorise the advice. The acronym he chose was PHONE.

P:	**Prepare:**	have any facts or information to hand; make sure you know who you wish to speak with; have pen and paper handy to make notes.
H:	**Hello:**	introduce yourself and your organisation; ensure that you are speaking to an appropriate person.
O:	**Obvious:**	speak clearly; make the purpose of your call *obvious*; *listen* carefully; if necessary, ask questions to clarify what the other person is saying.
N:	**Note:**	make a careful and accurate note of anything important, particularly names and numbers – read these back to the other person to check their accuracy.
E:	**End:**	end the call politely and thank the other person for their help.

Guidance

The chart and accompanying sketch are intended to support the points about using the telephone. The image should be clear and relevant (PC1); suited to the audience and purpose (PC2); and displayed in an appropriate place, e.g. beside the telephone (PC3).

PRACTICE

CONSIDER whether information may be more effectively communicated by using a chart, or other image, that can express the information clearly and concisely.

 HELP
If you need help in using images, turn to page 116.

 EVIDENCE
Assignment 17 (page 77) provides an opportunity to produce evidence of achievement in presenting information clearly.

19 Anna Young writes a report and makes a presentation

When carrying out the survey of customer satisfaction with Clare Delaney, Anna was particularly interested in customers' replies to question 13b: How much do you like the colour of the shop?

Most customers liked the colour scheme very much or much, which led Anna to consider the importance of colour schemes to customers' levels of satisfaction. She decided to write an assignment for her GNVQ course on the use of colour in business and to make a short presentation on the topic. First of all she read some material given to her by Remedy staff which referred to colour, then she made a library search at her college to find a book that dealt more generally with the topic of colour use by businesses.

Anna used **keyword** search and used the words **customer, satisfaction**, and **care** to come up with a number of titles of books that might deal with the topic. She then scanned through the books, using the contents pages and indices (plural of index), until she came across information about the use of colour in a book entitled, *The Psychology of Customer Care*, written by James Lynch (Macmillan, 1992). She skimmed through this book until she found the information she needed in order to understand why Remedy used certain colours for different parts of its shops and for the packaging and display of particular goods.

Guidance

When seeking information for an assignment or a presentation it is wise to make use of the catalogue system of a library. This will help you to find what you need quickly. Ask the librarian if you need help in using the catalogue – explain what you are looking for and make notes on how to use the system.

 PRACTICE

WHEN you read background materials for reports and presentations, it is often a wise strategy to scan through until you find something relevant; then skim-read more closely; and finally study particular passages that you think will be of use. Try to have a clear question or focus in mind when you read a book – it will help you to read efficiently. Take notes and summarise the information you need.

 HELP
If you need help to read efficiently, turn to page 125.

 EVIDENCE
Assignment 23 (page 78) provides an opportunity to produce evidence of achievement in reading to research a subject.

Writing notes

Anna made notes when reading the materials she had been given by Remedy or had borrowed from the library, and then summarised them:

PHARMACY

Colour scheme: grey and green. Grey is a passive colour which creates a clinical, technical atmosphere. On its own it would be too cold so it is blended with green to create a sense of health and environmental friendliness.

Pharmacy products are often packaged in colours that echo these colour tones, although all colours may be found; for example, orange to give a sense of energy (vitamin pills); yellow to attract attention.

BEAUTY AND PERSONAL CARE

Colour scheme: grey and gold. Grey is used once again to give a sense of technical proficiency and a certain clinical tone to some product ranges. It is blended with gold to create an up-market sense of wealth and luxury which fits in well with some of the beauty products.

Beauty and personal care products are often packaged in colours that reflect these colour tones; for example, gold tops to perfume bottles give a sense of opulence; red creates a strong physical image in some lipsticks (which have names to match, like Raunchy Red).

BABY PRODUCTS

Colour scheme: yellow, pink and light blue. These colours are warm in tone and create the right atmosphere in which to shop for girls' and boys' clothes. Yellow can encourage impulse buying but is also unisex; pink creates a 'caring', feminine image but can be too sugary on its own; light blue is a calm colour and is associated with baby boys.

The use of colour in baby products matches this colour scheme. Some products, intended primarily for little boys, carry a lot of light blue; products for little girls have a lot of pink; and, more popular than either, are unisex products in various pastel shades, often with yellow tones, such as lemon or cream.

Source: *The Psychology of Customer Care* by James J. Lynch, Macmillan Press Ltd, 1992.

Guidance

Brackets or parentheses are used here because the information about the names of lipsticks is additional and not strictly relevant to the rest of the paragraph about colour.

Guidance

Anna has used words like 'passive', 'clinical' and 'environmental'. English is a very rich and complex language, with many alternative words to express fine shades of meaning. The use of a dictionary and a thesaurus can help you to use language with precision.

▶ **PRACTICE**

Report writing is a task that is often called for in industry, commerce and education. To become skilled at writing reports, you need to take any opportunity that your GNVQ course presents to practise this talent.

 HELP
If you need help in writing reports, turn to page 98.

 EVIDENCE
Assignment 14 (page 77) provides an opportunity to produce evidence of achievement in writing a report.

Images to illustrate the presentation

Guidance

Images can greatly enhance an assignment report or presentation. In this particular case, photographs will make the subject more vivid to an audience than other forms of image, such as sketches.

To accompany her presentation, Anna decided to take some photographs. She asked Judith Argyle's permission, who, in turn, had to ask the Managing Director of Remedy, Eileen MacQuarry. Eileen thought it a good idea and donated a slide film, together with processing. Anna then took a few photographs of areas of the shop and of different products to illustrate her assignment and the presentation she intended to give.

Anna Young makes the presentation

Guidance

Prepare carefully for presentations but do not overprepare so that you become stale. If in doubt, try it on a friend first. Use notes to jog your memory but never read aloud for more than a few moments because this can be very tedious for an audience.

Guidance

Making presentations is often nerve racking, even for experienced speakers, especially to people, like fellow students, whom you know well. Adequate preparation and a few simple breathing exercises are all it takes to overcome nerves.

During the presentation Anna will try to:

- keep to the subject of the presentation (PC1);
- speak in a tone and manner suited to the audience and situation (PC2);
- listen attentively to any contributions from the audience and show that she has understood them (PC3);
- ask questions or summarise points to take the discussion forward (PC4).

In preparation for her presentation, Anna made some notes to jog her memory about what she wishes to say, but she did not read from them directly. Instead, she glanced occasionally at her notes to remind herself of what she wished to say next.

At suitable points during the presentation, Anna showed the slide photographs that she had taken of the colours used in various parts of the shop and in the packaging of products.

 PRACTICE

EITHER alone, or with one or more people, give a talk or presentation on a topic of your choice. Prepare the talk with care so that the needs of the audience are considered. Try to follow all the Performance Criteria for TAKE PART IN DISCUSSIONS.

Use suitable images to illustrate the presentation and decide in advance how and when you will use them.

 HELP
If you need further help in making a presentation, turn to page 98.

 EVIDENCE
Assignment 3 (page 75) provides an opportunity to produce evidence of achievement in talking to a group of people.

20 The staff party

Meeting to discuss the party

Linford Andrews decided that it would be morale-boosting to have a staff party. The first thing he had to do was to enlist the support of senior staff, like Judith Argyle and the Managing Director, Eileen MacQuarry. To prepare for this, he gathered his thoughts about a party, trying to anticipate the questions he might be asked. He made a few notes.

PROPOSAL FOR A STAFF PARTY

Why have a party?   Have a good time
Boost staff morale
People get to know each other better

What sort of party?   An eating, drinking, dancing party –
something for everyone

When?   Friday or Saturday night, eight 'til late
Soon

Who will it be for?   All staff and their partners – pharmacists,
managers, sales staff, cleaners

Organised by?   Me, plus helpers

Cost?   To be worked out – but will be kept as low as
possible
A small donation from Remedy would be
welcome

Guidance

If a meeting is important, and the people involved busy, it is wise to do some advance preparation so that the meeting can be focused and reach its objectives quickly. People often jot down ideas as a means of thinking through an issue. The notes may then be redrafted into a neater, more readable format, perhaps on an index card.

 PRACTICE

JUST as Linford Andrews made notes, make preliminary notes of the main points to be discussed at a meeting you will attend, e.g. with a tutor, an employer, an experienced employee in your GNVQ area. Then summarise the notes into a clearer and more logical form for the meeting. Write the final draft on a card or small sheet of paper that you can use during the meeting to jog your memory.

 HELP
If you need more help to make notes, turn to page 126.

 EVIDENCE
Assignment 7 (page 76) provides an opportunity to produce evidence of achievement in making notes for a meeting.

Linford knew that the meeting to discuss a staff party, although relatively informal, needed to be focused. His preparation persuaded Eileen and Judith that he had thought through the main issues and could be trusted to organise the party. The Managing Director offered to subsidise the arrangements for the staff party by donating £100 and by allowing Linford to use time and the telephone to make the arrangements. She was concerned that the party should be well attended and should not make a loss and agreed with Linford that he must keep careful check of the finances and make sure that the party was well advertised among staff. She asked Judith Argyle to be closely involved in planning the party.

 PRACTICE

ATTEND a meeting for which you have already prepared. Before the meeting, make notes of how you will behave.

After the meeting review how you think it went. Are you happy about your performance, or do you think you need to develop your skills?

At LEVEL 3 it is important to practise talking about complex matters to people who may be unfamiliar with the subject matter. Try to estimate how much they will know already; choose your words with care, avoiding difficult or technical terms, or explaining them.

 HELP
If you need more help in talking and listening, turn to page 85.

 EVIDENCE
Assignment 2 (page 75) provides an opportunity to produce evidence of achievement in attending a meeting.

The memo to confirm arrangements

Guidance

This is a typical memo (short for memorandum, a note to help the memory). The layout is in a standard format which, in many organisations, is preprinted. All the writer has to do is fill in the names and date and write the information or request as briefly as possible. It is not necessary to sign a memo.

To ensure that what was agreed at the meeting is clear, so that problems later on can be minimised, Eileen MacQuarry sent Linford a memo, with a copy to Judith Argyle. The memo is brief and to the point:

TO	Linford Andrews
	Judith Argyle
FROM	Eileen MacQuarry
DATE	14 April
SUBJECT	The staff party

Thank you for offering to organise a staff party. Please go ahead and book a venue and a disco and arrange catering and drinks. As agreed, you will take full responsibility for the financial planning and accounting for the event and will not delegate this. Please liaise closely with Ms Argyle. Thanks again for this initiative.

The purpose of a memo like this is to ensure that what has been agreed is clear. In particular, the Managing Director was concerned that the party should not lose money and that Linford Andrews should keep personal control of this aspect. The language is therefore brief and to the point, without being threatening.

PRACTICE

USE any opportunity that presents itself to write a memo or minutes, summarising what was agreed at a meeting. Try to write briefly and plainly so that there is no ambiguity or doubt.

 HELP
If you need help in writing memos, turn to page 97.

 EVIDENCE
Assignment 10 (page 76) provides an opportunity to produce evidence of achievement in writing a memo.

Using the telephone to book a venue

Guidance

When using the telephone we do not have the usual range of clues to know how the other person is reacting to what we say. We can't see their eyes, their facial expressions, or their body posture. In consequence, we sometimes feel uncertain and even nervous. To help overcome this prepare to use the telephone by making notes. Try to relax and talk in a normal voice, at a normal pace.

Linford Andrews wishes to hire a hall for the party. He needed information about a number of halls: size, capacity, licensing for music and dancing, costs, dates available, etc. He had a number of options.

- He could write to a number of halls – in which case he would need to wait for replies and then might need to write again to clarify points.
- He could visit a number of halls – but this is time consuming and they might be shut, or the person he needs to talk to may not be there.
- The most efficient way to contact the halls is to use the telephone.

Unless he holds the names and numbers of halls on file, the next step would be to use *Yellow Pages* or another local telephone guide. Under the word *Halls* he will find a list of possible venues for the dance from which to select a few to contact.

He would then telephone a number of halls (say, six) to obtain the information he needs, making a note of their replies, together with their name and telephone number.

Use images: a table

In order to record information clearly and simply, Linford may draw up a simple table, like this, which itemises the information he needs to know.

Hall	Tel	Capacity	Licence?	Kitchen	Cost	Dates

He may need to call back to talk to someone who has the information he needs or to check further details. Eventually, he will be ready to make a decision and to send a letter to confirm a booking.

 PRACTICE

MAKING a telephone call: choose a topic about which you need information. It may be connected with your GNVQ (e.g. the cost of purchasing particular items of equipment; the availability of local work placements) or with your personal life (e.g. the costs and times of alternative forms of travel to a particular destination; the cost of a particular CD system).

Write notes about the information you need and use a table to record the information you obtain.

Reading: Consult *Yellow Pages* or another local directory and search for suitable

Guidance

Most directories have sections at the front and/or back which explain how to use the directory. Most are arranged in alphabetical order. The best way to get to know a directory is to **use** it.

For some searches in *Yellow Pages*, e.g. CD, it may be necessary to consult the *Classification Index* at the back for alternative sections, e.g. **Computers**: *peripherals* or **Audio Dealers**: *TV, video & radio shops*. In case of real difficulty it is possible to phone *Talking Pages*, but there may be a charge for this service.

numbers. Telephone directories are used routinely in all organisations and follow a preset format, therefore their use is at LEVEL 1.

Make notes of important points discussed during the call.

HELP
If you need more help in using the telephone, turn to page 92.

EVIDENCE
Assignment 4 (page 75) provides an opportunity to produce evidence of achievement in using the telephone.

The letter of confirmation

Once Linford Andrews had agreed by telephone to book a hall, he decided to write a brief letter of confirmation so that both he and the hall staff have a record of the agreement.

Here is Linford Andrew's letter.

Guidance

- Business letters should be as brief as possible, while including all necessary information. (PRODUCE WRITTEN MATERIAL: PC1).
- The letter should be typed or written legibly (PC2).
- Standard conventions of grammar, punctuation and spelling should be followed (PC3).
- The letter should be organised to maximise the reader's understanding – in this case the purpose of the letter and key information are stated in the first paragraph. Further paragraphs go into more detail. The letter ends politely (PC5).

In this case the letter is at LEVEL 2 because the hall manager, for whom the letter is written, is familiar with the subject; and the subject matter is routine.

The High Street, Dover DO1 2XZ

18 April 199_

James Macpherson
Hall Manager
New Hall
Excise Road
Dover DO7 7YT

Dear Mr Macpherson,

Hall Booking

Following our recent telephone conversation, I am writing to confirm a booking of the Hall on 23 May, 7 p.m.–2 a.m. at the agreed price of £120.

As you know, we intend to hold a staff party and would therefore like tables and chairs to be arranged round the edge of the hall, with the central area free for dancing.

The disco has its own sound system but will need power. We will set up a bar, using volunteer helpers, who will need washing up facilities. As agreed, we will bring our own glasses and washing materials and will clean the bar area and kitchen after use.

Thank you for your co-operation in helping us to organise the event.

Yours sincerely,

Linford Andrews

Linford Andrews
Shop Accounting Controller

Use images: a sketch

Linford Andrews drew a simple sketch to show the hall manager how he wishes the hall to be laid out, and attached this to the letter.

Guidance

The sketch satisfies the Performance Criteria for Element 2.3: Use images. It illustrates clearly where Linford Andrews wishes the tables placed (PC1). Although it is roughly drawn, it suits its purpose and will be understood by the hall manager (PC2). It is appropriate to attach it to the letter so that it may be detached and given to the staff who will set out the tables (PC3).

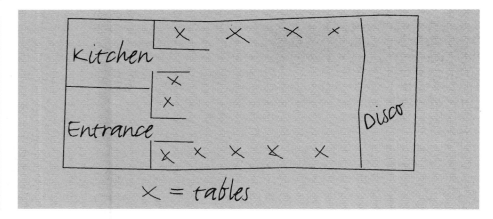

▶ PRACTICE

WRITING brief, informative business letters takes practice. Be patient. Draft letters, show them to a friend for comment. How easily can they be read? Are they clear?

Use any real opportunity to write business letters (e.g. a letter to your bank manager requesting an overdraft; a letter to an employer asking if there is any part-time work available). Keep all letters and replies to use as evidence of achievement.

When you write or speak to people, consider whether at any point it would be helpful to use an image, such as a simple sketch.

 HELP
If you require help with the layout of a letter (e.g. where to place addresses, dates) or the conventions of letter writing (e.g. when to use sincerely or faithfully), turn to page 97.
If you need help to use images, turn to page 116.

 EVIDENCE
Assignment 12 (page 76) provides an opportunity to produce evidence of achievement in writing a letter.

The memo to staff

Linford Andrews decided to send a memo to each member of staff, asking for their help in organising the staff party. He decided that a memo would be more effective than a notice which may be read by some people only. Judith Argyle asked Linford Andrews to let her see a draft of the memo because she was concerned that the tone of the memo should be appropriate – she did not want it to sound too pressing and, at the same time, she did not want people to be distracted from their work.

Here is the draft of Linford Andrew's memo.

> Dear Colleague,
>
> I am writing to let you know that we are thinking of having a party so that we can get to know everyone better and at the same time all have a good time. I am sure you have now guessed what this letter is about – can you spare a little time to help?
>
> I realise how busy you are but if you can spare some time to help, please let me know.
>
> Best wishes
>
> etc.

Offering advice

If you were Judith Argyle, would you suggest any amendments to this memo before it is sent to staff?

Judith Argyle made a number of suggestions in notes on the memo.

> I like the letter and think its tone is about right.
>
> I think you should point out that partners and friends are invited too.
>
> Rather than just letting you know, I think it would be a good idea to hold an informal meeting for volunteers, with tea and biscuits, one evening after work.
>
> Dear Colleague,———— We have a list of staff on computer so can we use people's actual names, rather than 'Dear Colleague'?
>
> I am writing to let you know that we are thinking of having a party so that we can get to know everyone better and at the same time all have a good time. I am sure you have now guessed what this letter is about – can you spare a little time to help?
>
> I realise how busy you are but if you can spare some time to help, please let me know.
>
> Best wishes etc.
>
> Can the letter be clearer about the sort of help needed? Something like, 'serving behind the bar, providing some food for a buffet, helping to clean the hall after the dance'?
>
> As the decision to have a party has been taken, perhaps you should say 'I am organising' rather than 'thinking of having'.
>
> You use 'time' with different meanings in the same sentence. How about 'enjoy ourselves' rather than 'have a good time'?

Judith's reading and response is at LEVEL 3, because she is making judgements about the suitability of Linford's memo and needs to deal with it sensitively. Linford read the suggestions and did not feel offended by

Guidance

Feelings can hinder understanding. Whether reading or listening, it is easy for our feelings (pride, anger, resentment, etc.) to get in the way of understanding. Linford could have thought, 'How dare she criticise my letter!' and, as a result, might almost have ignored her suggestions.

them because he had drafted the memo quite quickly and knew that Judith's ideas were meant to be constructive – another person can often see straightaway what a writer may miss entirely.

Linford read Judith's notes and extracted the following four main points (READING: PC4):

- the memo should be personalised;
- its use of language should be improved;
- the help needed should be stated clearly;
- a meeting of staff should be held.

 PRACTICE

READ material that is sent to you and try to be aware of how your feelings can sometimes interfere with your comprehension. In fact, understanding is often a combination of thought and feeling but if feelings overwhelm thought, much can be missed.

 HELP
If you need help in extracting information from your reading, turn to page 125.

 EVIDENCE
Assignment 26 (page 79) provides an opportunity to produce evidence of achievement in reading and responding to other people's writing.

Redrafting the memo

Linford rewrote the memo, incorporating Judith Argyle's ideas.

The High Street, Dover DO1 2XZ

23 April 199_

Dear [Name of person],

I am writing to seek your help. I am organising a party for staff and their partners and friends, so that we can get to know each other better and at the same time enjoy ourselves. I am sure you have now guessed what this letter is about – can you spare a little time to help?

I realise how busy you are but if you will, for example:

- spend some time behind the bar
- provide some food for a buffet
- help to clean the hall after the party

it would be much appreciated.

If you think you can help in any way, please come along for a cup of tea and an informal meeting in the staff room on 29 April when the shop closes.

Best wishes,

PRACTICE

REREAD one or two letters or memos that you have already written and redraft them to improve:

- what you have written – can anything unnecessary be taken out? Can anything be added to improve the letter's accuracy or clarity? (PC1);
- the legibility of the handwriting, or spacing, typeface and typesize (PC2);
- the spelling, punctuation and grammar (PC3);
- the organisation of the letter or memo, and your choice of words, in order to make it easier for the reader to understand (PC5).

Whether the letter is at LEVEL 2 or 3 will depend on how complex (or sensitive) the subject is, and on how familiar the audience is, both to you and with the subject matter.

 HELP
If you need help with any aspect of letter writing, turn to page 97.

 EVIDENCE
Assignment 11 (page 76) provides an opportunity to produce evidence of achievement in redrafting material.

The informal meeting for volunteers

Prior to the meeting, Linford Andrews drew a simple chart of tasks, in order to help staff to see at a glance what help is needed.

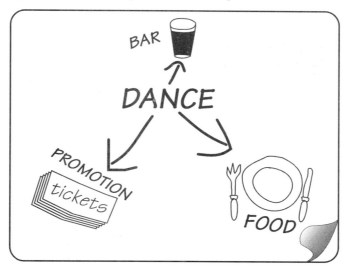

Guidance

The chart is simple but effective, using few words and images for maximum effect.

 PRACTICE

PREPARE for a meeting by drawing up a list of the points that you think should be covered. Use images, if appropriate, to make these points clear. The meeting does not necessarily have to be one arranged by you. Your points could refer only to those things that you, personally, think are important.

Attend the meeting and try tactfully to raise and deal with the points on your list. Remember to follow the Performance Criteria for TAKE PART IN DISCUSSIONS:

- Make contributions which are relevant to the subject and purpose (PC1).
- Make contributions in a way that is suited to the audience and situation (PC2).
- Listen attentively and confirm that you have understood the contributions of others (PC3).
- Make contributions which take the discussion forward (PC4).
- At LEVEL 3, create opportunities for others to contribute (PC5).

HELP
If you need help in handling meetings, turn to page 93.

If you need help in handling meetings, turn to page 93.

E V I D E N C E
Assignment 7 (page 76) provides an opportunity to produce evidence of achievement in preparing for a meeting.
Assignment 20 (page 78) provides an opportunity to produce evidence of achievement in using an image to illustrate a discussion.

Designing a poster and tickets for the staff party

Linford Andrews asked Anna Young if she would produce designs for a poster and for tickets that could be duplicated on a photocopier. Anna's initial reaction was that she could not draw anything suitable, but Linford encouraged her.

Here is Anna's attempt at designing a ticket.

Guidance

The tickets and the poster both have two functions – to communicate information, and to encourage interest in the staff party. Sometimes too much information can reduce interest, so it may be necessary to keep information to the essentials. With much design work the saying 'less matter, more art' should be borne in mind.

The poster

Linford Andrews wanted a simple poster which could be put up in the staff room. Here is Anna's attempt.

Guidance

You do not have to be a skilled artist to produce simple sketches to illustrate your work nor to use layout to enhance meaning. Easy-to-use computer packages can assist you to produce images that will illustrate points you wish to make in speaking or writing, and images to give you ideas are readily available in books and magazines.

PRACTICE

U SE any opportunity that presents itself to use layout to enhance meaning, and to use sketches or other images to illustrate and aid communication.

 HELP
If you need help in using images, turn to page 116.

 EVIDENCE
Assignment 17 (page 77) provides an opportunity to produce evidence of achievement in using layout to enhance communication.

21 Anna Young's letter of thanks

Anna wrote a letter of thanks to Remedy for taking her on on work placement. She decided to address the letter to the Shop Manager, Judith Argyle, and to thank by name individuals who had been particularly kind and helpful to her. Here is Anna's first draft of the letter:

> 40 Old Farm Road,
> Dover
>
> Dear Ms Argyle,
>
> Thanks for having me on placement. I had a really great time and made lots of friends. It helped my course a lot and I have decided to try to get into retail management as a result. Please give my best regards to Clare Delaney and Mr Andrews. They were both really helpful and I appreciated it.
>
> Yours faithfully,

Anna showed the letter to her GNVQ tutor who thought that the letter was cheerful and polite but could be improved. He made a number of suggestions. In summary, the suggestions were that:

- the letter could include some more information about what was found useful about the placement;
- the meaning could be made clearer in places;
- the use of standard conventions could be improved;
- paragraphing would help the structure of the letter;
- the style should be a little less chatty.

As a result of the tutor's feedback, Anna redrafted the letter. Here is her second draft:

Guidance

Most writers need to draft and redraft in order to express themselves clearly. The constructive suggestions of other people can be very helpful to a writer.

Redrafting

40 Old Farm Road,
Dover
DO4 6BS

11 May 199_

Ms Argyle,
The Manager,
Remedy,
47 The High Street,
Dover DO1 2XZ

Dear Ms Argyle,

I am writing to thank you and your staff for taking me on work placement. People were very kind to me and I should like to thank, in particular, Mr Andrews and Clare Delaney.

My experience benefited my GNVQ coursework and gave me a useful insight into the way that business operates. As a result of what I learned, I wrote an assignment about the importance of customer care, and gave a presentation about the use of colour in retailing.

I think that retail management may suit me and so I have decided to apply for a job in a company like Remedy which offers training. Thank you once again for allowing me to spend time with Remedy and please give my very best wishes to everyone I worked with.

Yours sincerely

Anna Young
GNVQ student, Drucker College

► PRACTICE

THERE may be occasions when you need to write a work-related letter which, at the same time, has a personal touch. For example, you may write a letter of thanks to people who took you on work placement; or to staff who helped to make your holiday enjoyable. Remember to be warm and sincere.

HELP
If you need help with letter writing, turn to page 100.

EVIDENCE
Assignment 12 (page 76) provides an opportunity to produce evidence of achievement in writing a letter.

22 Judith Argyle gives a talk to a GNVQ group

Following her placement, Anna Young phoned Judith Argyle to ask if she would give a talk to the GNVQ group on a topic of Judith's choice. Judith offered to talk about 'The Importance of Staff Training and Morale in Achieving Business Excellence', a subject she already intended to research in order to write an article for the Remedy in-house staff magazine, *Remedy News and Views*.

Judith Argyle carries out research

Guidance

When searching for materials for an assignment or presentation it helps to have a clear idea of what you're looking for. Judith wanted information on staff training and morale, so she searched using headings like *staff training, human resource planning,* and *the retail industry.* Be prepared to use a range of alternative words in order to find what you are looking for.

Guidance

Here Judith has quoted directly from a publication. She has used inverted commas to show that it is a direct quotation and has made a careful note of the source. The dots ... indicate that Judith edited out a section of the original.

For these summary notes, Judith has read a section of a book (Barnes, S. *Essential Business Studies* and has *paraphrased* it, using some of her own words, and some words from the original.

Guidance

Judith selected suitable materials for her purpose (READ AND RESPOND: PC1); extracted the necessary information from them (PC2); used appropriate sources of reference to clarify her understanding (PC3); and summarised the information she extracted (PC4).

To prepare for writing the article for *Remedy News and Views* and for giving her talk to the GNVQ group, Judith used a library and books of her own to search for relevant background materials.

Judith discovered a number of books and articles that covered aspects of the subject of staff training and morale. She **scanned** these looking for relevant sections which she **skimmed** for useful information. Finally, she read some parts in detail and made summary notes. Here are some of her notes:

"Human resource managers are ... 'people strategists' and facilitators who are tightly integrated members of the management team. This fits in with the growing idea of more flexible, proactive organizations that are less hierarchical and bureaucratic." Source: Barnes, S., <u>Essential Business Studies</u>, Collins Educational, 1994.

Conflict in organizations may have many symptoms, such as high staff turnover, absenteeism, accidents or customer complaints. Conflict can lead to low efficiency and a slowness to react to change. The underlying reasons for conflict may include:

* rigid and authoritarian management with a lack of bottom-up communication, causing a build-up of frustration

* rapid or poorly planned change

* decline in market share, causing the threat of redundancy

* lack of involvement, boredom or alienation

* badly designed organizational structure

Rehearsing the talk

Guidance

The importance of an image: Maslow's use of a triangle helped to show that human beings have a hierarchy of needs, from basic bodily or physiological needs to needs for self-fulfilment. Unless the lower levels are met, it is not possible to move on to the higher levels.

Judith organised what she wished to say into clear headings on separate cue cards. She intended to use these as prompts, not to read from them. Here are some of her headings:

Good training doesn't cost; it pays
Conflict in organizations has many symptoms, such as high staff turnover, absenteeism, accidents or customer complaints
Poor service is often the fault of the company, e.g., insufficient training

Using the cue cards, Judith rehearsed the talk, making a note of the time it took because she wanted to leave plenty of time for questions and discussion. She decided that she would take questions at any time during the talk, and made a note to herself to mention this at the beginning.

Use images

Guidance

The use of overhead transparencies can be a great help in presenting a subject, but they should not be overused. They should be legible, even from the back of the room, and should not contain too many words to read.

To illustrate the talk, Judith decided to use some images, including Abraham Maslow's triangle. She put this on a transparency to use on an overhead projector.

From this Judith drew the conclusion that to motivate people at work it is necessary not just to pay them and provide a decent working environment, but also to meet their needs for respect and for personal fulfilment. Work should not be a meaningless and boring experience.

Giving the talk

During the talk Judith tried to:

- keep to the subject (DISCUSSION PC1);
- fit what she said (e.g. in vocabulary, tone and manner) to the audience of GNVQ students (PC2);
- check that she understood the points that people made (PC3);
- keep the discussion moving forward (PC4);
- make sure that everyone joined in the session (PC5).

She did this by a variety of means, such as:

- preparing properly;
- telling people that she wanted them to ask;
- listening and responding appropriately to what people had to say;
- keeping good eye contact with everyone, so that she could spot and draw in the quieter students.

EVIDENCE OPPORTUNITIES

Gathering evidence of achievement

Evidence of achievement may be gathered from:

- previous education and experience;
- work carried out for any GNVQ or NVQ unit;
- work carried out on any other education programme (e.g. GCSE, A level, A/S level);
- experience outside education (e.g. in a part-time job, a hobby, a club, etc.).

Assignments and projects

In practice, on a GNVQ programme, you will carry out assignments and projects that cover a number of elements, or even a number of units, simultaneously. For example, you may read books that contain images, in order to prepare a handout that you will give to people as part of a presentation. The elements of Communication are inter-related, like this:

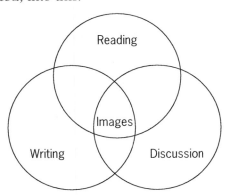

For the purpose of assessment, however, it may be necessary to break down what you have done, in order to show that you have satisfied the performance criteria for the particular elements of Communication.

Cover all relevant performance criteria

Whatever the source of evidence, it is essential that it covers all the relevant performance criteria for an element of Communication. For example, if you cite a discussion you took part in as evidence for ELEMENT 2.1 OR 3.1: TAKE PART IN DISCUSSIONS, it is necessary to show that you have satisfied *all* the relevant criteria – you can't claim that your contributions have been relevant (PC 1) if, for instance, you have not listened to and understood what other people have said (PC 3). If the criteria are applicable to a particular activity, you must satisfy them all, and show evidence that you have done so.

Cover all parts of range

The range statements show, for each element, what sorts of subjects, audiences and situations you must deal with in communicating.

Audience

In order to show that you can use a variety of styles of speaking, writing and using images to suit the needs of different people, it is necessary to communicate with a range of audiences:

At level 2 and 3:
- people familiar with the subject who know you
- people familiar with the subject who do not know you

At level 3:
- people unfamiliar with the subject who know you
- people unfamiliar with the subject who do not know you

Record the type of audience for each activity to ensure that you cover the range necessary.

In the assignments that follow, it is sometimes clear what kind of audience is involved, and sometimes it is up to you to involve people from outside your group, in order to ensure that you have experience of communicating with different audiences.

Presenting your evidence to an assessor

At the beginning of your GNVQ programme you should make sure that you are clear about who will assess your work. Often you will be taught by a number of people, and it is the responsibility of those teaching you to make plain to you the arrangements for assessment. **If you are not clear, ask**.

The more well organised you are in presenting evidence of achievement, the more you will help assessors to make reliable judgements about your work. This in turn will help you to learn and to develop.

Take part in discussions

Evidence of achievement should be given in ways that enable an assessor to make a reliable judgement. For you to say, 'I covered ELEMENT 2.1: TAKE PART IN DISCUSSIONS by talking to customers in a shop last Saturday', without actually showing some evidence (e.g. a letter from the manager that refers to how you covered the performance criteria, and a tape recording of you talking to customers) makes it impossible for an assessor to make a judgement.

In practice, it is often easier to gather evidence when the assessor is actually present, i.e. during your GNVQ course, when activities and projects are set up specifically for you to practise and show what you can do. So, for example, you may be observed by an assessor while you are taking part in discussions.

Produce written material and produce images

Evidence of writing, and using images, can be collected in a portfolio of documents. It must be evident that this is all your own work, that it shows coverage of all the performance criteria, and that it covers the range.

The portfolio should contain a variety of formats of writing (e.g. letters, reports, notes); and a variety of images (e.g. photographs, charts, sketches – some of which you will have produced yourself for a particular purpose).

Read and respond to materials

Evidence of reading may be more difficult to gather, and it may be necessary to keep a log of all books and articles that you have read, that also shows how you have *used* and *responded* to your reading.

Liaise with an assessor before you embark on your reading; keep careful records of everything you read; make notes of the key points you discover; keep a careful record of how you have used your reading (e.g. to write a report, prepare a presentation, etc.).

Don't forget that you need to gather evidence of reading and responding to images (e.g. charts, graphs, tables, maps) as well as written materials.

Summary of how to record achievement

Some of the ways you may gather evidence of achievement are by keeping:

- a portfolio of written material (letters, memos, reports, etc.);
- a portfolio of images used;
- a log of people spoken to, perhaps divided into telephone calls, discussions with individuals, and presentations to groups of people;
- a record of all books and articles read, and how you used this reading in your assignments, etc.

Whatever types of recording you use, it is essential to show how the *performance criteria* for the particular *level* you wish to achieve have been satisfied, together with the requirements of *range* (e.g. that you have spoken with and written to the full range of audiences).

Suggestions for assignments

Here are suggestions for assignments to improve your performance in Communication and to help you build a portfolio of evidence of achievement. These assignments may supplement those you will complete as part of your GNVQ course.

The assignments are organised in six sections:

- four sections contain assignments that relate to each of the four elements – so that you may focus on developing a particular skill (pages 75–79);
- two sections contain assignments that cover a number of elements for LEVEL 2 (pages 79–81) and for LEVEL 3 (pages 81–83).

When you have completed an assignment successfully, tick the box and write in the date, as a reminder.

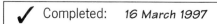
✓ Completed: *16 March 1997*

Take care to record your achievement in the documents provided on your GNVQ course.

Assignments for Element 1: Take part in discussions (levels 2 and 3)

Level: whether a discussion is at LEVEL 2 or LEVEL 3 depends on the complexity of the subject and the nature of the audience. Complex, non-routine matters, requiring careful use of language to make meaning clear, and discussions with people unfamiliar with the subject are at LEVEL 3. If you are in doubt, consult the assessor in advance.

1. Take part in one-to one discussions

> Completed:

Use any opportunity that occurs on your GNVQ course to take part in discussions with other people. Review the performance criteria for discussions and try to ensure that you listen and respond, as well as speak.

If an assessor is not present, you may have to record the meeting on audio or video tape to provide sufficient evidence of your contributions (see *Recording the voice* on page 95).

2. Attend a meeting

> Completed:

Use any opportunity that occurs on your GNVQ course or in your outside life to attend a meeting with one or more people (e.g. with a teacher, job-placement employer, local Careers Officer).

Prepare for the meeting in advance by making some notes. Contribute appropriately and review your speaking and listening against the Performance Criteria for TAKE PART IN DISCUSSIONS.

If an assessor is not present, you may have to record the meeting on audio tape or video tape to provide sufficient evidence of your contributions. (See *Recording the voice* on page 95).

Make notes after the meeting to summarise the main points that were discussed. If the meeting is a formal one that is minuted, obtain a copy of the minutes.

3. Speak to a group of people

> Completed:

Use an opportunity that occurs on your course or in your private life to give a talk to a group of people.

The talk or presentation may be quite brief (10–15 minutes) and should be prepared by making brief notes (to jog your memory, *not* to read from). It may be illustrated by the use of appropriate images. Leave time after your talk for a discussion of some of the issues raised. Adjust what you say to how much the audience will know about the subject.

Retain your preparatory notes for the talk. The talk should either be attended by someone who can assess you, or should be video- or audio-taped so that it can be assessed later. (See *Recording the voice* on page 95.)

Obtain feedback

It would be useful, if possible, to ask your audience to complete an *Evaluation Sheet* at the end of your talk (see page 94).

4. Use the telephone

> Completed:

Keep a written record of all telephone calls you make that may satisfy all the Performance Criteria for the level you require:

- keep the notes you make to prepare the call;
- keep the notes you make during and after the call;
- make a tape recording of your speaking during two or three calls to use as evidence that you satisfy the Performance Criteria for ELEMENT 2.1 or 3.1. (See *Recording the voice* on page 95).

5. Review communication problems

> Completed:

During discussions there will be occasions when people do not communicate harmoniously or effectively – for example, there may be disagreements; or a complaint may be made or responded to inappropriately; or someone may give a talk that is not understood by the audience. You may learn from these occasions. Consult *The Help Section* on *Take part in discussions* (pages 85–95) and review the ineffective discussion. What can you learn from what happened?

Write a brief report.

Assignments for Element 2: Produce written material (levels 2 and 3)

Level: whether written material is at LEVEL 2 or LEVEL 3 depends on the complexity of the subject and the nature of the audience. Complex, non-routine matters, requiring careful use of structure and style to make meaning clear, and materials produced for people unfamiliar with the subject, are at LEVEL 3. If you are in doubt, consult the assessor in advance.

6. Handle sensitive situations

Completed:

Review situations that you have experienced when sensitivity to the feelings of others was important. How well did people behave? Were there ways of handling the situation more effectively? Write a summary account.

Imagine sensitive situations that may arise in school, college or a workplace (e.g. misunderstandings; health problems; bereavement). How well do you think you would handle them? What skills or personal attitudes would be important in dealing with the situation? Write a summary of how you might behave.

7. Notes for a meeting

Completed:

Prepare notes for a meeting. Consider the subject of the meeting and the nature of the audience (e.g. how much they will know about the subject). It may be a good idea to include an image (e.g. a diagram, a table, a graph) in order to be able to support a point you wish to make. Keep the notes in a portfolio, together with a record of the meeting.

8. Minutes of a meeting

Completed:

Agree to take notes at a meeting (e.g. an assignment planning meeting; a club meeting) and write the minutes of the meeting, following the guidance given in *The Help Section* (page 100).

9. A flipchart sheet

Completed:

Produce a single flipchart sheet, illustrated by a suitable image, to display as part of a presentation.

You may have to research the subject (e.g. by consulting people; reading material). Make sure that the sheet is legible, even from the back of the room. Write it in a way that makes the subject as clear as possible to the readers, especially if they are unfamiliar with the subject. Check the spelling, punctuation and grammar.

10. A memo

Completed:

Write a memo to a member of staff or to people on your course, confirming details of an agreement or arrangement that forms part of preparations for a group assignment.

11. Drafting and re-drafting

Completed:

When you produce a piece of written work, ask a friend to comment on it positively and then re-draft it, taking account of their comments.

12. A letter

Completed:

Write a letter to an individual you do not know, or to a firm, requesting information about a subject of direct relevance to your GNVQ. Ensure that the layout of the letter is suitable; state the subject in the opening paragraph; keep the letter as brief as possible, while covering all relevant points; check spelling, punctuation and grammar.

13. A handout

Completed:

To provide information to people (e.g. as part of a presentation, or as background to a project) produce a handout of key points. You may be able to produce some photocopies (not necessarily one per person).

14. A report

Completed:

Research a topic that is part of your GNVQ (e.g. by consulting people; reading books and articles). Make notes of any relevant material. Summarise your notes in the form of a written report, supported by images. Set out the report to a length and format agreed in advance with your tutor or assessor (e.g. use sub-headings, numbering or lettering to organise material); when you write the report, bear in mind who the audience will be, and how much they will know about the subject; check the spelling, punctuation and grammar.

15. An article

Completed:

Write a short article for a school/college/company newspaper or magazine; or for a local publication. It may be necessary to research the subject (e.g. by consulting people; reading material). Make notes of any relevant material. Summarise your notes in the form of an article, perhaps supported by images. Set out the article in a way that will maximise audience interest and understanding (bear in mind how much they will know about the subject) to a length agreed with the editor. Check spelling, punctuation and grammar.

Assignments for Element 3: Use images (levels 2 and 3)

Level: whether images are at LEVEL 2 or LEVEL 3 depends on the level of the written or spoken communication they support. If you are in doubt, consult the assessor in advance.

16. Photographs

Completed:

Take photographs (prints or slides) or reproduce professionally produced images to illustrate a talk on a subject of relevance to your GNVQ. Make sure that the pictures illustrate clearly the points you wish to make, and will be understood by the audience. Use them at an appropriate time during the talk. Ensure that the audience can see slides (even from the back of the room) or have time to examine prints. Keep a record of your images and how you used them.

17. Use layout to enhance communication

Completed:

Use layout to enhance the meaning and impact of a document (e.g. a poster, notice, leaflet or form). Use one or more images, either from source material, such as books and magazines, or that you have produced yourself to suit the particular purpose of the poster (e.g. to attract attention, arouse interest, convey information). Check the spelling of any words used. Consult other people about the effectiveness of the poster for its purpose.

18. Present statistical information

Completed:

Select a suitable image (e.g. graph, table, pie chart, bar chart or pictogram, etc.) to present figures about a subject relevant to your GNVQ. Choose an image that will present the information as clearly as possible, given the subject and the particular audience (e.g. how much will they know about the subject?). Make a record of how you used the image (e.g. in written material or a discussion) and how effective it was in communicating the information.

19. Design a flow chart

Completed:

Design a flow chart to show how a sequence or process works (e.g. the production and distribution of goods) or the interconnection of ideas (e.g. stress at work and health). Use the flow chart to illustrate a presentation or an assignment.

20. A sketch

Completed:

Draw a sketch to illustrate written material or a discussion. The sketch may be very simple (e.g. using matchstick people) as long as it serves the purpose intended (e.g. to communicate information; introduce some humour; arouse people's interest). Maximise the effectiveness of the sketch by using it at an appropriate time during a discussion, or at a suitable point in a document. Keep the sketch and a record of how you used it.

21. Draw a map

Completed:

Draw a map for someone who is not familiar with the area. It should be accurate, while being straightforward to read. Give the map a sense of scale and include a few landmarks or other features to help orientate the reader. Check on its use to see that it is suitable in practice.

Assignments for Element 4: Read and respond to materials (levels 2 and 3)

Level: whether reading material is at LEVEL 2 or LEVEL 3 depends on the complexity of the subject. Complex, non-routine materials, requiring careful reading and judgement for full understanding, are at LEVEL 3. If you are in doubt, consult the assessor in advance.

22. Select professionally produced images

Completed:

It is sometimes more effective to select an image from materials (books, magazines, newspapers, etc.) than to produce images yourself. Professionally produced images are often clearer and their use may save time. When preparing for written work or discussions, try to find appropriate images that illustrate the points you wish to make. Use the images in accordance with the performance criteria for USE IMAGES.

23. Research in a library

Completed:

Use a library to investigate a topic of interest to you (see *The Help Section*, page 122) that is directly linked to your GNVQ, or to a hobby or other personal interest. Make notes of the information you discover, using a card index or similar system for storing and retrieving information. Record the name of each author and the title, publisher and date of publication of each book or article consulted. Remember that reading is not a one-gear activity – use contents pages and bibliographies; scan and skim, in order to extract efficiently the information you need.

Summarise the information you have extracted, either in writing or orally, and keep a copy of your summaries.

24. Use appropriate sources of reference

Completed:

From time to time you will come across parts of written material that you will not understand, and you must be able to show that you can use appropriate sources of reference. At LEVEL 2, sources of reference will be provided for you; at LEVEL 3 you may have to find them yourself. Sometimes it is best to ask another person for help (e.g. a tutor, another student) and at other times you may have to consult books, such as a dictionary, thesaurus or encyclopedia. Use the reference section of a library and consult a range of reference materials. Ask a librarian for help in finding the most suitable references. Keep a note of the sources you use and how you use them.

25. Compare newspaper reports

Completed:

When a subject of relevance to your GNVQ is in the news, study the ways in which several national newspapers deal with it.

Judge the relevance, fullness and accuracy of each newspaper's coverage and write a brief report that may be used to make a presentation to your group.

26. Read and comment on other people's writing

It can be helpful to read drafts of other people's work (and to have people read and comment on your draft work). When reading and commenting on others' work, be sensitive to their feelings – remember the sandwich method of giving advice (praise; offer helpful criticism/feedback; praise and encourage). It may be helpful to write a summary of the main points you wish to make for the other person to refer to.

27. Understand images

Completed:

From time to time in your reading you will see images (e.g. symbols, charts, sketches) that convey information. Write notes on these to show that you have understood them.

28. Read and respond to images that present statistical information

Completed:

The reference section of most libraries contains a number of publications that present statistical information (e.g. about government departments; companies; countries) in the form of tables, graphs, charts, etc. Search for relevant statistical information on a topic connected with your GNVQ. Read the images, making notes of any information that is relevant to your purpose (e.g. to prepare for a discussion; to write a report). As with other written materials, use a card index or similar system for storing and retrieving information. Record the name of each publication with its publisher and date. Don't forget to use appropriate sources of clarification (e.g. a tutor, a librarian) to help you understand the images.

Combined assignments for level 2

Level: there is no reason why LEVEL 3 students should not complete these assignments, adding to them as appropriate to cover all the performance criteria for LEVEL 3.

29. Apply for a job

Completed:

Write your own Curriculum Vitae (CV). It does not have to be for an actual job, although it helps to have a specific job in mind that might be feasible to apply for (have a look through local and national newspapers, or magazines relevant to your GNVQ area, to get an idea of a relevant job to apply for). Read about writing a CV in *The Help Section* (page 99), and prepare by making notes about what you will write, and then draft the whole document before typing or writing the final version as neatly as possible.

Write an application letter to accompany the CV – consult *The Help Section* first (page 100).

30. Research two competing products

Completed:

Select two competing products. Find out as much as you can about them (e.g. price, durability, market penetration, advertising, packaging, etc.). Consumer reports (such as those produced by *Which?*) may be helpful.

Write a short report about the products, illustrating it with images, such as photographs and sketches, as appropriate.

Based on your report, give a short (e.g. 10–15 minute) talk to your class, illustrated with some images, and use a simple feedback sheet (see *Obtain feedback* on page 94) to obtain an evaluation of your performance.

31. Design a questionnaire

Completed:

Design a questionnaire to investigate a specific, straightforward topic – perhaps agreed in advance with your tutor/assessor. The topic may be connected with your GNVQ or may be about general issues (e.g. the holiday, eating or leisure preferences of a group of people). The people questioned may be your fellow learners, family and friends, or members of the public.

You may have to telephone one or more people to obtain permission to use the questionnaire (e.g. if you wish to go into private premises to question members of the public).

Be realistic about the length of the questionnaire – people may not be able to give you a lot of their time; and about the number of people you can question in the time that you have. Read about questionnaires in *The Help Section* (page 102) before drafting your questions. Test the questionnaire on two or three people before preparing the final version.

Once you have had the questionnaires returned to you completed, analyse the results, taking care to interpret them honestly and not to put your own bias on the results.

Write a short report that describes the topic you investigated and the results of the survey (include a copy of the questionnaire as an appendix). Bear in mind who the report is for. Use images, such as tables and charts, to illustrate the report.

Based on your report, give a short (e.g. 10–15 minutes) talk to your group. Invite people from another group to attend. Illustrate your talk with some images. Leave time after your talk for a discussion of some of the issues raised. Use a simple feedback sheet (see *Obtain feedback* on page 94) to obtain an evaluation of your performance.

32. Investigate an organisation

Completed:

Select an organisation or an operating unit of an organisation (e.g. retail outlet, marketing department, sports centre, etc.). Decide on a specific topic you wish to find out about (e.g. what customer services are provided; access for disabled people; health and safety issues, etc.).

Use the telephone to arrange a visit during which you can talk to an appropriate member of staff about the topic you wish to investigate. Request some information in advance (e.g. leaflets) if it is easy to provide (you should offer to send a stamped addressed envelope).

Prepare for the visit by using a library to consult relevant books or articles on the topic (see *Using a library* on page 122). Draw up a checklist of questions you wish to ask.

Make the visit, and discuss your questions with a member of staff at the organisation. Make adequate notes of the meeting or, if possible, tape the meeting, with the permission of the member of staff.

After the visit, read your notes or playback and make notes from the tape. Write a short report about the facility, illustrated with appropriate images.

Write a letter of thanks to staff you talked to at the organisation. Enclose a copy of your report, if your tutor thinks it appropriate.

Based on your report, give a short (e.g. 10–15 minutes) talk to your group. Invite people from the facility to attend. Illustrate your talk with some images. Leave time after your talk for a discussion of some of the issues raised, and use a simple feedback sheet (see *Obtain feedback* on page 94) to obtain an evaluation of your performance.

33. Observe a reception area

Completed:

Read the part of *The Help Section* about speaking and listening to people (pages 85–95). Use a library to read books and articles about the skills needed to organise and run a reception area (see *Using a library* on page 122).

Telephone an organisation (e.g. local company, hospital) to request to spend some time (perhaps two half-days) observing the way the reception area works. Be specific about the sorts of things you wish to learn (e.g. record keeping, appropriate behaviour, telephone manner, etc.). You may have to put your request in writing. If so, write a letter to confirm your visit.

When you make your visit to the reception area, introduce yourself and explain what you hope to observe. Remember to dress and behave appropriately for a reception area. Observe, ask appropriate questions, discuss issues with the staff and make notes of the things you learn.

After the visit, read your notes and write a short report that states where you went, what you observed, and comments on any features of the use of communication in the reception area that you found interesting. The report may be illustrated by appropriate images, including a diagram showing the layout of the reception area.

Write a letter of thanks, both to the reception staff and to the organisation. Enclose a copy of your report, if your tutor thinks it appropriate.

Based on your report, give a short (e.g. 10–15 minutes) talk to your group. Invite people from the reception area to attend. Illustrate your talk with some images. Leave time after your talk for a discussion of some of the issues raised, and use a simple feedback sheet (see *Obtain feedback* on page 94) to obtain an evaluation of your performance.

34. Observe people speaking and listening

Completed:

Read the part of *The Help Section* about speaking and listening (pages 85–95) and make notes about the main features to look out for when observing people holding conversations. Draw up a checklist (you may want to concentrate on particular aspects of speaking and listening, such as eye contact, tone of voice, choice of vocabulary; or you may want to include many features).

Select particular situations and observe people speaking and listening. For example, you may observe adults speaking with children in a nursery; staff talking with elderly people in a residential centre; teenagers discussing an issue in a refectory. In some instances, you may have to obtain permission to observe, by telephoning and/or writing to discuss the project.

Make notes during the observation – possibly by recording a particular behaviour each time it occurs. If you can obtain permission to tape the situation, and the use of a video or tape recorder does not distort the conversation too much (i.e. people do not change their behaviour because they know they are being recorded) this may help you observe more closely.

After your observations are complete, review your notes (and tapes if you have them) and write a short report about what you have learned about the ways in which people speak and listen in particular situations. Take care to ensure the anonymity of people observed by referring to them as fictitious names or as letters (person A, person B, etc.). Illustrate the report with appropriate images (e.g. a table of results; a diagram of body language or layout of a room).

Based on your report, give a short (e.g. 10 minute) talk to your group, inviting people from other groups who may be interested. Illustrate your talk with some images. Leave time after your talk for a discussion of some of the issues raised. Use a simple feedback sheet (see *Obtain feedback* on page 94) to obtain an evaluation of your performance.

Combined assignments for level 3

Level: LEVEL 2 students may attempt these assignments. So long as all LEVEL 2 performance criteria are covered, they may produce evidence of achievement.

35. Investigate non-discriminatory practice

Completed:

Read the part of *The Help Section* about uses of language that avoid discrimination against disabled people, women, and members of ethnic minorities (page 90). Carry out some background research in a library to consider what effects discrimination may have on people's health and well-being, and their access to education and employment.

Investigate two different kinds of facilities or organisations in your locality (e.g. retail outlet; cinema; college) to see what measures they take to avoid discrimination and encourage access. Try to focus your enquiry upon specific issues (e.g. use of mission statements; training of staff; wheelchair access, etc.).

Telephone to discuss and arrange a visit to your selected organisations, sending a follow-up letter of confirmation if necessary.

Devise a simple questionnaire or checklist of questions to help you find out the information you seek. Remember that discrimination is a potentially sensitive subject to investigate. Be tactful and sensitive in your questioning.

Visit the organisations to talk to people and discuss the issues about non-discriminatory practices that you wish to focus on.

Write a report, illustrated with suitable images, that sets out your findings and that maintains the anonymity of the organisations and individuals who participated.

Write letters of thanks to the people who co-operated in the project. Enclose a copy of your report, if your tutor thinks it appropriate.

Based on your report, give a short talk to your group. Invite people from the organisations to attend. Illustrate your talk with some images. Leave time after your talk for a discussion of some of the issues raised, and use a simple feedback sheet (see *Obtain feedback* on page 94) to obtain an evaluation of your performance.

36. Investigate the effect of Information Technology

Completed:

Identify one or two organisations in which to investigate the effect of IT on working practices (e.g. local company, legal practice, college). Telephone to discuss and arrange a visit, possibly sending a follow-up letter of confirmation.

Carry out some background research to prepare for your visit (see *Using a library* on page 122). Devise a simple questionnaire or checklist of questions to find out the information you seek.

Visit the organisations to talk to people and discuss the aspects concerning the use of Information Technology that you wish to focus on.

Write a report, illustrated with suitable images, that sets out your findings and also maintains the anonymity of the organisations and individuals who participated.

Write letters of thanks to the people who co-operated in the project. Enclose a copy of your report, if your tutor thinks it appropriate to do so.

Based on your report, give a short talk to your class. Invite people from the organisations to attend. Illustrate the talk with some images. Leave time after your talk for a discussion of some of the issues raised. Use a simple feedback sheet (see *Obtain feedback* on page 94) to obtain an evaluation of your performance.

37. Investigate team work

Completed:

Read the part of *The Help Section* about speaking and listening (page 85), especially those aspects, such as *Establishing and maintaining rapport* (page 86), that are particularly important to working in teams. Use a library to do some background reading and make notes on teams and team building (see *Using a library* on page 122).

Identify one or two organisations (e.g. a hotel, a local firm, a school) in which you could investigate the issue of effective teamwork. Telephone them to discuss what you wish to do and to arrange access. It would be wise to send a letter confirming arrangements.

Based on your background reading, prepare a simple questionnaire or checklist of questions about effective teamwork. Visit the places with which you have made arrangements and talk to people there about their perceptions of teamwork.

Write a report, illustrated with suitable images, that sets out your findings and that maintains the anonymity of the organisations and individuals who participated.

Write letters of thanks to the people who co-operated in the project. Enclose a copy of your report, if your tutor thinks it appropriate.

Based on your report, give a short talk to your group. Invite people from the facilities to take part. Illustrate your talk with some images. Leave enough time after your talk for a discussion of some of the issues raised. Use a simple feedback sheet (see *Obtain feedback* on page 94) to obtain an evaluation of your performance.

38. Investigate the influence of external factors on an industry's performance

Completed:

All sectors of industry are affected by a range of external factors – government policy, economic performance, levels of world trade, wars, changes in people's expectations, etc. Choose the industry that you are interested in and investigate the factors that have affected it the over the past 5 years, and the factors that you think are likely to affect it in the next 5 years.

Carry out a library search, making use of trade publications, newspapers and journals, as well as books (see *Using a library* on page 122).

Telephone or write to a few key people in the industry in your locality (e.g. a customer services manager, a personnel manager, a tourist facility operator) to arrange to interview them about their perceptions of external factors. Draw up a checklist of questions to ask them, based on your reading.

Write a report, illustrated with suitable images, that sets out your findings and that maintains the anonymity of the organisations and individuals who participated.

Write letters of thanks to the people who co-operated in the project. Enclose a copy of your report, if you tutor thinks it appropriate.

Based on your report, give a short talk to your group. Invite the people you interviewed to take part. Illustrate your talk with some images. Leave time after your talk for a discussion of some of the issues raised. Use a simple feedback sheet (see *Obtain feedback* on page 94) to obtain an evaluation of your performance.

39. Plan an event

Completed:

Working with others, plan an event (e.g. a sponsored walk to raise money for charity; a visit to a place of interest; a dance). Negotiate roles in the team to cover all aspects of planning for and organising the event, to include, for example:

- making telephone calls and writing letters to make preliminary arrangements, obtain permissions, find out information;

- ensuring adequate health and safety provision for the event;
- advertising and publicity.

Keep a record of all team meetings, particularly of decisions made and who will carry them out. Make notes also of how the team operates. Who plays what role in the team? Do people really listen to one another and reach collective decisions? What aspects of communication should the team try to improve?

Hold the event.

Carry out an evaluation of the event, against criteria agreed in advance by the team. Evaluation may include feedback from participants at the event.

Keep a careful record of your own part in the planning, running and evaluation of the event and match this against the performance criteria for the Communication elements.

40. Investigate the layout of accommodation

Completed:

Telephone and/or write to negotiate access to one or more work places (e.g. offices, factories, retail outlets). Visit the work places and draw simple diagrams showing the layout of accommodation.

Evaluate the efficiency and suitability of the accommodation, taking account of the needs of potential users, including disabled people.

Return to the facilities to discuss your evaluation with staff. This will require tact and careful research on your part. Prepare for your visit by drawing up a checklist of issues and questions.

Write a report, illustrated with suitable images, that sets out the results of your investigation and that maintains the anonymity of the organisations and individuals who participated.

Write letters of thanks to the people who co-operated in the project. Enclose a copy of your report, if your tutor thinks it appropriate.

Based on your report, give a short talk to your group. Invite people from the work places you visited to take part. Illustrate your talk with some images. Leave time after your talk for a discussion of some of the issues raised. Use a simple feedback sheet (see *Obtain feedback* on page 94) to obtain an evaluation of your performance.

THE HELP SECTION

What is language?

Language is a constantly changing human attribute, and the English language is now spoken throughout the world by about a thousand million people.

Language is not only about communicating with others. Much of our thinking is carried out in language and we 'talk to ourselves' from time to time to clarify our thoughts.

However, the main purpose of language assessed as a core skill is communication: the use of language to express and understand information, opinions and instructions. Through language we interpret and understand the world, as well as transmit ideas about it.

Speaking and listening are natural human activities and most people cannot avoid becoming very skilful at an early age. Writing and reading, however, are skills that we have to learn and, like all skills, they can be improved by practice.

Images are used in writing and speaking to illustrate points, and sometimes – for example, if two architects are discussing ideas – may almost take the place of words.

All four elements of Communication are inter-related:

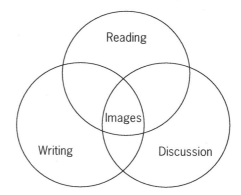

Failure to communicate effectively is the cause of much unhappiness and is estimated to cost billions of pounds a year due to stress-related illness causing absence from education and work. In a democratic society, it is essential that people express their views and respect those of others – people who cannot communicate effectively may become the victims of those who can.

Element 2.1 and 3.1: Take part in discussions

SPEAKING AND LISTENING

The ease or difficulty of speaking and listening depends mainly on three factors:

- what is being spoken about

- who you are speaking to

- whether you are speaking face to face or on the telephone

Even young children talk differently to a friend, a parent and a teacher. By the time people are in their teens, most have a wide repertoire of language styles to fit particular situations.

STOP AND THINK
Think about times when your own style of speaking may change (e.g. in an interview; making a presentation; talking to a baby; talking to a foreigner who speaks little English).

It is important that you use the appropriate style for the situation. For instance, it is not a good idea to shout at an interview; and it may not be appropriate to speak softly and slowly, choosing your words with care, at a football match.

Style is affected by a number of factors, including:

- The situation in which the language is being used – for example, are you making a formal presentation, or having an informal chat?

- The subject that is being communicated – is it complex (e.g. technical, scientific, sensitive) or straightforward?

- The audience for which you speak or write – how well do you know your listeners or readers? How much do they know about the subject?

The manner in which you speak refers to the fact that, 'It ain't what you say, it's the way that you say it'. Manner involves observing social conventions which are appropriate to the situation, and speaking in an appropriate tone of voice. Our tone changes according to different situations, and it is made up of a number of factors including:

- Pitch – we tend to talk with a higher or rising pitch when excited, talking to babies, or asking questions.

- Loudness – we tend to talk more loudly to people we suspect may not understand us.

- Speed – we tend to talk more quickly when we get excited, or feel nervous.

STOP AND THINK
Make a note of the different ways of speaking used by you, your friends and family. Under what circumstances do you alter the way you speak?

Grice's maxims

Paul Grice (1975) reasoned that conversation is based on a cooperative principle, built upon four maxims:

- *Quantity*: say neither too much nor too little. Be as informative as you need to be.

- *Quality*: say only what you believe you can show to be true.

- *Relevance*: keep to the topic.

- *Manner*: express yourself clearly and in an orderly way, avoiding jargon and ambiguity.

If a maxim is broken (e.g. if someone rambles on, lies, wanders from the point, or deliberately uses obscure words) there may be an attempt by the listener to 'mend fences' and assume there is a good reason for the speaker to talk in that way. If there is not a good reason, the speaker may come to be regarded as a bore or labelled a liar.

Sometimes people deliberately break a maxim for fun, or because the principle of cooperation comes first. If someone intends to borrow a pen and you answer their question, 'Do you have a pen?' with 'Yes, thanks', it may be that you are deliberately flouting maxim 3: Relevance. Jokes are often based on breaking the 'rules' of language. The art of storytelling deliberately breaks maxim 2: Quality, by sometimes inventing fabulous lies. Very honest people may lie or equivocate so as not to hurt people's feelings; the ugly-baby syndrome requires that we sometimes bend the truth so as not to hurt people. This is known as 'tact' – an intuitive understanding of the appropriate thing to do or say.

Underlying Grice's maxim is the rule that helps people to co-exist: be polite. Robin Lakoff (1977) suggested three rules for politeness:

1) Formality: neither impose nor remain aloof.

2) Hesitancy: give people spoken to room to express their own views; don't box people in.

3) Equality or Camaraderie: act as though you and the person you are talking to are equal. Make the other person feel good.

Underlying all these 'rules' are two even more fundamental ones: be yourself (self-respect) and be sincere (respect the other person).

The right to speak

Each person has a unique voice, which is why when an old friend telephones, even after years of separation, we recognise the person by the voice. Everyone has a right to speak, and we have a responsibility to listen to what other people have to say.

There is evidence that men – especially white, middle-class men with 'educated' South-East England accents – dominate in many speech situations. In doing so they may discourage others from speaking. Men in general have tended to speak, in public situations, more than women, whereas women have been more likely than men to express their thoughts and ideas with friends and colleagues.

A voice specialist, Patsy Rodenburg (*The Right to Speak*, 1992, Methuen) thinks that British society does not encourage people to express themselves freely. She recounted working at Eton where she was 'stunned by the open vocal release and freedom', compared to working in a comprehensive in a depressed area of London where, 'Discussion was minimal. It was rare...it was all just slightly short of vocal repression.'

 STOP AND THINK
Reflect on your own speaking and listening. Do you ever intimidate? Are you ever intimidated?

Reflect on your words
Cooperative social life is based upon being self-conscious or reflective about the effect our words and actions have upon other people. A dog can communicate by, for example, barking or wagging its tail, but these gestures are not self-conscious in the way that human communication can be. If I poke out my tongue to a friend she may laugh; if I poke it out to a stranger on a train he may take offence. A dog will bark at anyone if it is in a barking mood. Some human beings behave in this way too, saying or doing things without fully comprehending the effect on other people. In very young children this may be acceptable but as people grow they are expected to be more sensitive and aware of others.

Verbal bullying
The saying 'Sticks and stones will break your bones but words will never hurt you', is untrue. What people say – or fail to say – can hurt other people very deeply. It is possible to bully, sometimes in subtle ways by, for example, making disparaging or sarcastic remarks or by inappropriate responses (e.g. laughing, sneering, looking away) in order to 'put down' another person. Often bullies have themselves been bullied and show their fear and lack of self-respect by their behaviour. However, this does not diminish the hurtfulness of verbal bullying.

If you are being bullied, it is wise not to suffer in silence – be assertive, or talk it over with someone else.

Establishing and maintaining rapport

Rapport is about harmonious relationships between people. Sometimes you hit it off with another person straight away – there is a rapport between you, though it may be difficult to explain why. There are also people to whom you find it difficult to relate.

In working situations we have to get on with all sorts of people. It is important that, without being shallow or insincere, we try to smooth relationships, to establish as much rapport as we can, because by doing so everyone's life is more pleasant and work tasks are accomplished more easily.

One good way to establish and maintain rapport is to give people time, listen to them, talk to them. Often you will discover that you have some common ground after all (rapport is often established by talking about subjects that interest both people).

Finding common ground with another person is often about establishing what experiences and interests you share. This is the reason why the weather is often used as a conversation opener. When people are in love they often talk about themselves because the other person is fascinated by just about anything they say. Normally, however, we must try a little harder to find the common ground.

Working in teams

Both in employment and domestic life, it can greatly facilitate tasks and the well-being of individuals if people collaborate and act in teams, rather than behaving as isolated individuals. Much has been written about the roles people play in teams (e.g. leader, coordinator, clown, outsider, etc.) and the stages that teams may go through as they come together, carry out their task and then disintegrate (e.g. forming, storming, 'norming', performing and mourning). Underlying all successful teamwork is the ability of a number of people in the team to communicate effectively. There are no magic formulas about how to do this – no two teams are identical – but much of what is written in this help section about speaking and listening is of importance to individuals who wish to contribute to successful teamwork. It is also important to document team meetings accurately (see *Documenting a meeting*, p.101).

Listening skills

One of the most important skills for communicating well is the ability and the willingness to listen. Possessing ears does not automatically make people good listeners.

 STOP AND THINK
Take it in turns with another person to talk about a subject that interests you (e.g. a holiday, a film). For the first two minutes the listener should pay attention, then they should 'switch off' for two minutes, and finally, should listen again. Swop roles and repeat the exercise.

The effect of listening behaviour is to help establish a feeling of harmony between people, even if they disagree about what is being said. It is inevitable that people will disagree about all sorts of subjects, but they can often do so in ways that enable them to find a basis for discussion and some common ground.

The effect of non-listening behaviour is to make the speaker feel a variety of negative emotions – wounded pride, humiliation, anger, resentment.

How can you tell if someone is listening or not?

Listening behaviour	Non-listening behaviour
Eye contact – not all the time but enough to show attention and interest	Too little eye contact (e.g looking around the room, reading, staring into space)
Body posture – orientation towards the speaker	Physically turning away
Verbal cues – making encouraging sounds (e.g. 'Mhm, yes...I agree')	Saying little or nothing so that silence means inattention, or that you are just awaiting your turn to speak
Other cues – nodding in agreement, smiling encouragingly	Frowning, sneering, sniggering

How did the experience of not being listened to make you feel?

None of these emotions helps to promote healthy relationships.

It is particularly difficult to listen when someone is criticising you – it is easy to ignore what is said because of feelings of wounded pride or anger. Try to concentrate on *what* is said and not on who says it, how it is said or your own feelings.

Talking down to people

If you listen to a mother talking to a young baby, she will often use a type of question that she does not expect an answer to, but that is intended to encourage communication in smiles and sounds. Questions, such as 'Are you going to give me a big smile, are you?' are often said in a higher pitch of voice than normal, and with rising intonation at the end. If a mother said, 'Who's a lovely baby, then?' and the baby replied, 'Search me. What about the one over there?' she would be astonished – and would move on to real questions, that require a reasoned reply. 'Babytalk', as it is called, is important in establishing a close bond between parent and child (lovers too, often use a similar type of language for the same reason).

When adults talk to very old people, or to people with disabilities, they may be tempted to use similar forms of 'babytalk', even when the older person is perfectly capable of reasoned conversation. Listen to

you're a sweet old feller, aren't you!

When adults talk to very old people they may be tempted to use 'Baby Talk'.

this conversation, in which the helper talks with higher pitch than normal, and with rising intonation at the end of sentences:

Older person: I had a party.

Helper: You used to have a big party?

Older person: I don't feel old.

Helper: Oh you don't feel old?

This is not a normal conversation. The helper is talking down to the older person.

 STOP AND THINK
What sort of reply to the older person's first statement, 'I had a party', might be given in a normal, adult to adult, conversation?

If the helper had responded to the first statement adult to adult, appropriate replies may have been: 'What kind of party?', 'I love parties.', or 'I thought you were the kind of person to enjoy a good party!'.

However, instead of responding, the helper merely repeats the older person's statement in a different form. And, to make matters worse, when the older person then says, 'I don't feel old', the helper repeats that too, instead of saying something like 'I'm sure you don't' or 'You don't look old'.

The best way to encourage other people to talk is to listen and to respond appropriately. That is what a parent is encouraging a baby to do when making 'babytalk'; that is what we should all try to do when talking to other people, adult to adult.

MAKING AND RECEIVING COMPLAINTS

Most complaints can be dealt with by simple courtesy from both sides. Whether making or receiving a complaint try to avoid types of attacking behaviour that are likely to lead to antagonism rather than to the resolution of the problem. Attacking behaviour may involve sarcasm, anger, belittling and other ways of focusing on the feelings of people, rather than on the problem itself.

Making a complaint

Before making a complaint check your facts (e.g. are you sure there is a fuse in the plug? Are you being reasonable?).

Human communication is based on a principle of cooperation (see *Grice's maxims*) so most people find making a complaint rather embarrassing, even when they have solid cause. If you think you have a reason to complain, be assertive (see *Speaking assertively*):

- Ensure that you are speaking to someone who can deal with the complaint.

- State the complaint clearly, without necessarily blaming anyone.

- State what you want done (be reasonable).

There are times when you may be quite justified in being angry, and showing it.

When making a complaint, try to be neither aggressive nor timid. Speak in a tone and manner suited to any other conversation with the person being spoken to. Remember the old saying, 'You catch more with honey than with vinegar'. Nevertheless, there are times when you may be quite justified in becoming angry, and showing it. This should always be after you have tried other approaches, rather than as your initial reaction.

Receiving a complaint

The person receiving a complaint should listen attentively and, if necessary, check that they have understood what the complaint is about. Depending on the nature of the complaint, they should either investigate immediately or offer to do so as soon as possible.

Most workplaces have standard procedures (formal or understood) to deal with complaints that may include recording the complaint, and bringing it to a manager's attention if the complaint is serious, etc.

Most complaints can be effectively dealt with by listening and reacting straight away in a sensible manner, avoiding time-consuming form filling, and argument.

Speaking assertively

Assertive behaviour means behaving in a manner that recognises that both you, and the person you are speaking with, have rights and responsibilities. You both have a right to express your opinions, and this right comes with a responsibility to listen with attention and respect to what the other person has to say.

Assertive speaking and listening is neither aggressive (e.g. shouting, dominating, using sarcasm, not listening) nor timid (e.g. not daring to say what you feel, tolerating the other person's aggression).

Some of the characteristics of assertive speaking are:

- listening to the other person and being attentive to what they are saying;

- focusing on the matters being discussed, rather than on personal feelings (for example, saying 'I don't agree with that point', rather than 'I don't agree with you, you are pig headed');

- responding in a tone and manner suited to talking to a fellow human being (i.e. with respect – shown by appropriate pitch, loudness, speed, etc.);

- if appropriate, saying no to a request, without necessarily giving a reason;

- maintaining your opinions, and your right to hold them, without backing down or forcing them on the other person;

- changing your opinion, agreeing with the other person, if there are grounds for doing so;

- owning your opinions by saying 'I think', rather than, 'they say', 'people think', 'it's common sense' or 'everyone knows that ...';

- praising people and showing positive pleasure when this is what you feel, without being patronising.

AVOID BIAS AND DISCRIMINATION IN YOUR USE OF LANGUAGE

It is possible, even without knowing it, to offend other people by your use of language. Try to be sensitive to the feelings of other people. In particular, avoid stereotyping people by lumping them all together in big groups that are supposedly all alike (e.g. people with disabilities, women, ethnic groups). People are unique individuals. No two are alike, and like you, they are all susceptible to feeling patronised or insulted. Put yourself in the other person's shoes. How would the words you use strike you? Remember, it is not true that 'words will never hurt you'.

While trying to be aware of other people's feelings, don't go too far and use unhelpful terms such as, for example, 'visually challenged' when you mean 'partially sighted'.

Gender

For thousands of years, in many societies, women have been treated as subordinates to men. Their voices were not expected to be heard on important matters. Men did not take kindly to being contradicted by a woman, and women were not always listened to as attentively as men – men 'talked', women 'gossiped'. Some terms may be positive when applied to men but negative when applied to women (e.g. 'ambitious'). These days men and women are more aware of this systematic discrimination and are more prepared to watch out for the ways in which it may be perpetuated in language.

Whether speaking or writing, the word 'he' or 'his' is often used to mean an unspecified person of either sex. This can have the effect of excluding women (e.g. 'When an old friend telephones we recognise him by his voice', may not produce an image of a woman as well as a man). Sometimes the problem can be avoided by using a different sentence structure (e.g. 'When an old friend telephones we recognise who it is by their voice); sometimes by using she *and* he, although this is rather clumsy (e.g. 'When an old friend telephones we recognise him or her by his or her voice'). If you cannot avoid a gender-specific pronoun use 'he' if you are male, and 'she' if you are female.

Nearly half the people in employment are women and they have all sorts of jobs, but there are still many gender-stereotyped words used (e.g. 'foreman' rather than 'supervisor'; 'air hostess' rather than 'cabin staff'; 'chairman' rather than 'chair').

Avoid using belittling terms such as 'bimbo', 'toy boy', 'hen-pecked', 'girls' to refer to grown people.

Use similar terms of address for men and women. Call everyone by their first names or their surnames; if you don't know the name of a person you are writing to, or can't use a general term (e.g. 'Dear Colleague', 'Dear Customer') then use 'Dear Sir/Madam'. Women may prefer to be addressed as Ms rather than Mrs or Miss (Mr does not show marital status).

Ethnic groups

Everyone belongs to an ethnic group that shares similar characteristics of geography, history, culture, religion, and so on. In Britain there are many ethnic groups (e.g. White, Afro-Caribbean, Asian). The groups can be sub-divided (e.g. White: English, Scottish, Welsh, Irish). Even these can be further divided (e.g. English: Londoners, Cornish, Liverpudlians). As you break down the groups you realise that the terms are just very simplified ways of grouping people who, as individuals, are very different. There is no such person as a typical Londoner, let alone a typical White, Afro-Caribbean or Asian.

So, avoid using language that lumps many people together and ignores their individual humanity. If you wish to refer to a group of people then try to be as precise as possible. Don't use 'English' or 'England'

when you mean 'British' or 'Britain'. When referring to minority ethnic groups, avoid using 'Black' when you mean 'Afro-Caribbean' or 'Asian'.

Try to avoid the use of 'black' in derogatory contexts (e.g. 'black marks', 'black spot', 'black sheep'). However, it is acceptable to use black as a normal adjective (e.g. 'blackboard').

Disability

One person in seven in Britain has a disability. That's over 6 million people, and you cannot lump together that number of people as one homogeneous mass. Once again, try to treat people as individuals or, when referring to a group, try to be as precise as possible (e.g. use 'partially deaf' or 'profoundly deaf' as appropriate, rather than just 'deaf', and 'blind' or 'partially sighted' as appropriate.

Avoid inaccurate and insulting terms (e.g. use 'people with Down's Syndrome', not 'Mongols'; 'people with Cerebral Palsy', not 'Spastics').

People with disabilities are no braver or more 'pathetic' than anyone else. They succeed because of their abilities, not because they are necessarily courageous. They are entitled to access to public facilities and other features of everyday life, such as employment and housing, without being patronised. They should not be talked down to, because most are capable of holding their own in any conversation.

Age

Older people, too, can be lumped together by insulting terms such as 'old dear' or 'old fogey', when most of them are perfectly fit and able. Most human characteristics are not age related – you can be a 'fogey' (behind the times) at any age.

Sexual orientation

The term 'homosexual', first used in 1869, has been the standard term to refer to people who are physically attracted to their own sex. The term has so often been used as one of abuse or discrimination that people who are homosexual have promoted the term 'gay'. 'Lesbian' is an acceptable term to refer to homosexual women.

Avoid terms that have often been used in a demeaning way, such as 'queer', 'dyke', although some homosexual people may use these terms themselves.

Use the term 'partner', rather than 'spouse', because some people live together without being married. Some married people also prefer 'partner', rather than 'husband' or 'wife', although most married people probably find 'husband' and 'wife' perfectly acceptable.

STOP AND THINK
Are there any occasions when you show bias or discrimination against other people in the language you use?

THE SOUNDS OF ENGLISH

There are two main types of syllables: vowels and consonants. The English vowels are a, e, i, o, u. Any letters of the alphabet that are not vowels are examples of consonants. A consonant is a speech sound in which the breath is partly obstructed (e.g. by the tongue).

Accents

People are often self-conscious about the way that they speak, believing for example that they talk with the 'wrong' accent for the setting.

Everyone has an accent. Received Pronunciation (sometimes called 'Oxbridge' or 'BBC') is only one accent among many in English, and as a form of language it is neither better nor worse than any other accent. There is nothing wrong with an accent, as long as your communicating with other people is not hampered.

Be proud of your accent, but, if you think you have a problem with communication, or if you are self-conscious, you may do one or more of the following:

- Talk about accents with your family or friends. It is not a taboo subject: most people have thought about their accent at some time.

- Don't rush to change your accent – it is painful to hear someone trying too hard to talk in a way that is unnatural for them. Let your needs gradually change your accent over time.

- When you are nervous you tend to talk more quickly, and so emphasise your accent. So slow down. Talk at a pace at which you could sing the words.

Dialects

Groups of people sometimes use particular words or dialects to communicate with other members of the same group. A person from Yorkshire may call a total stranger 'love'; in Scotland a child may be called 'bairn'; and in Liverpool someone may say 'gissa' instead of 'give me'. The stronger the sense of group identity, the more likely it is that a particular dialect will be used. There are thousands of English dialects. They are associated with many factors, including:

- geographical area (e.g. Tyneside, Scotland)

- ethnic groups (e.g. Afro-Caribbean, South Asian)

- occupational groups (e.g. doctors, plumbers)

- youth culture (e.g. to describe clothes, music)

Some dialects change rapidly as they respond to constant shifts in people's ways of life. Sometimes, dialect expressions become part of standard English. For example, the Afro-Caribbean use of double negatives (e.g. 'There ain't no way'; 'Can't get no satisfaction') has become very widespread, partly through its use in music lyrics.

There is nothing wrong with using dialect in speech, as long as you can be understood clearly by your listeners. If you cannot be understood, it is not because your dialect is 'wrong' or because there is anything deficient with the understanding of the other person. It is usually simply that it can be difficult to tune-in to an unfamiliar dialect. It is up to you, as the speaker, to be aware of this.

For this reason it is important on occasions to be able to switch from dialect to a more standard English so that you can be understood in any circumstances you choose. This may be especially important when attending job interviews, where it is often expected that people will speak in ways that can be understood by other staff and any member of the public.

STOP AND THINK
If you think you have a problem with your dialect then follow the advice given in *Accents*.

NON-VERBAL COMMUNICATION

When we speak and listen we do not use only words, we also use a range of other means to communicate,

It is easy to jump to false conclusions about the meaning of a person's non-verbal communication.

such as sounds (e.g. 'mmm', 'oh', sighs), facial expressions, eye contact, body language, and the physical space we put between ourselves and others. ourselves and others. For example, the word 'no' can mean anything from 'yes' to 'maybe' to 'absolutely not', depending on how it is said and what body language accompanies it. It is extremely difficult to codify the huge number of variations of non-verbal language that arise in our interaction with other people. Be aware that it is easy to jump to false conclusions about the meaning of a person's non-verbal language. When we know someone well we can pick up subtle clues about their feelings from their non-verbal behaviour; with people we do not know well, especially if they are from a different cultural background, it can be difficult to 'read' their non-verbal behaviour accurately. If you want to find out more about this subject, carry out a library search.

USING THE TELEPHONE

When using the telephone we can't 'read' people's reactions in their eyes, posture and expressions. As a result we sometimes feel nervous. For this reason it is a good idea to gather your thoughts if you can before speaking.

Make notes if you are going to make an important telephone call (see *Making notes*). Try to relax. If you feel nervous you may talk too quickly (Let's get this over with) and talk incessantly (There mustn't be a moment's silence). Try to speak in a normal conversational tone, at a speed at which you could sing the words. Let the other person get a word in. Remember to say goodbye.

Answering a telephone call

Answering a telephone call can be almost as difficult as making a call. Remember to greet the caller appropriately: 'Hello', 'Good morning'. Give your own name or that of your organisation. Remember that tone of voice is particularly important when using the telephone. Try to sound relaxed, even if you are feeling tense. Speak at a normal speed and volume – try not to raise your voice or talk too quickly.

Make notes of any matters you wish to recall, especially if you need to pass a message to another person.

P: Prepare:
have any necessary facts or information to hand;
make sure you know who you wish to speak with;
have pen and paper handy to make notes.

H: Hello:
introduce yourself and your organisation;
ensure that you are speaking to an appropriate person.

O: Obvious:
speak clearly;
make the purpose of your call **obvious;**
listen carefully;
if necessary, ask questions to **clarify** what the other person is saying.

N: Note:
make a careful and accurate note of anything important, particularly names and numbers – read these back to the other person to check their accuracy.

E: End:
end the call politely, and thank the other person for their help.

Using an answerphone

Talking to a machine can be intimidating. Not only must you use the telephone, but you then have to relate to a disembodied voice. Don't be put off. Speak slowly after the tone, spelling any difficult words. Leave the following information: your name, the date and time of calling, what you are calling about, and a contact number. When leaving a number it helps to phrase it a few digits at a time so that the listener can write it down.

SPEAKING IN FORMAL SITUATIONS

When attending formal meetings (e.g. committees, interviews) or when making presentations, it is often helpful to prepare in advance.

Making notes

Many confident and experienced speakers prefer to have a few notes to help them talk on a topic, written clearly on index cards or sheets of paper. As you grow in confidence you may be able to speak 'off the cuff'. However, if you are unused to speaking to a group it is advisable to prepare notes and to follow them quite closely (see the section on *Making notes* on page 126). However, **do not just read straight from your notes – it will always sound stilted**.

Taking turns in meetings

It is often an unspoken rule that people will take turns to speak and to listen. It can be regarded as bad manners either to dominate discussion or to make too little effort to contribute.

It is a good idea to try to let everyone say something early in a meeting. The longer people stay silent, the more likely it is that they will say nothing for the whole meeting. There is some evidence that men tend to be more dominant than women in meetings – giving their views more often, and asking more questions – and that women listen more.

Encouraging people to contribute in meetings

It is important to ensure that everyone speaks who wishes to, and that no one dominates the discussion to the detriment of its purposes. A skilled chairperson in a formal meeting, and anyone skilled enough in an informal meeting, can help to encourage people to contribute by:

- knowing their names

- inviting people to introduce themselves

- inviting people by name to give their opinion

- thanking people for their contributions

And they can tactfully close down dominant people by thanking them for their contribution and inviting someone else to join in (e.g. 'Thanks for that. Would anyone else like to comment?').

Speaking to groups of people

Making presentations is often nerve racking, even for experienced speakers, especially to people, like fellow students, whom you know well. Adequate preparation and a few simple breathing exercises are all it takes to overcome nerves.

Make notes for a presentation, preferably one that you will actually have to make, either as part of your GNVQ or elsewhere.

- What could you talk about - make a list.

- What should you talk about (remember who you are talking to; what you are talking about; the attention span of your listeners, etc.).

- Gather or make a few simple images as visual aids to help you to illustrate the points you wish to make.

- Decide whether you prefer to answer questions during or after the presentation.

- Make the presentation. Review your performance. Did you:

- keep to the subject and purpose? (PC1)

- speak in a way suited to your listeners and the formality of the situation? (PC2)

- use images at appropriate times to illustrate points made more clearly? (Use Images: all PCs)

- listen attentively to the questions and contributions of others? (PC3)

- take the discussion forward by asking questions, summarising or otherwise responding to others' contributions? (PC4)

- explicitly encourage people to contribute and to ask questions (LEVEL 3: PC5)

It is helpful to try to find out in advance how much your audience will already know so that you do not bore them or talk above their heads. You should also bear in mind that people cannot concentrate on even the most fascinating speaker or topic for more than about 10 minutes before their minds begin to wander. As the saying goes, 'If you haven't struck oil in 10 minutes, stop boring'! Therefore:

- be selective about what you will say – don't try to make more than 4 or 5 different points;

- use some visual images (e.g. photographs, cartoons, or, if there are only a few people in your audience, objects to hand round) to keep the level of interest high.

Speaking to a group of people can be nerve-racking. Prepare adequately, but avoid over-preparation (it may make your speaking lack spontaneity); try to feel confident about your appearance, perhaps take a little more care about the way you dress; take a few deep breaths (e.g. 7-1-7 breathing: breathe in to a count of 7, hold your breath for 1, breathe out for 7).

When making a presentation, especially if there are many people present, it can be difficult to judge whether you are establishing rapport. A more conscious effort may be needed to decide whether people are listening attentively or have 'switched off'. The judicious (i.e. timely and appropriate) use of humour may help to enliven a presentation and keep the audience alert.

Some speakers like to begin with a humorous remark to gain the audience's attention, then use a little humour every few minutes to retain the audience's interest, and end with something humorous to leave the audience with positive feelings. However, if this is done in a mechanical way, or if humour is not appropriate, this can have a negative effect.

Obtain feedback

After a talk or presentation, it can be useful to ask the audience for feedback by, for example, completing an evaluation sheet like this:

Please comment on the following aspects of the presentation (please circle your responses):

How much did you know about the subject before the talk?

A lot   Quite a lot   Not much   Nothing

How well do you know the speaker?

Very well   Quite well   A little   Not at all

Organisation of ideas (evidence of background reading; logical structure, etc.)

Excellent   Good   Fair   Poor

Clarity of expression (choice of words, tone of voice, etc.)

Excellent   Good   Fair   Poor

Use of images (appropriate images, used at appropriate time, etc.)

Excellent   Good   Fair   Poor

Other Comments (e.g. mannerisms, length of talk, etc.):

Thank you for your comments

This feedback sheet provides information about the success of the talk and the nature of the audience – both of which are useful when gathering evidence of achievement.

Interviews

Interviews are potentially stressful situations. Whether you are being interviewed, or interviewing someone it is important to follow the advice in the previous sections, particularly about preparing by making some notes, speaking in an appropriate manner, establishing rapport, listening, being assertive, and avoiding bias and discrimination.

It is important to make people feel comfortable. Seating arrangements, dress and body language can either lead people to feel relatively relaxed or make them tense. If you wish to have a friendly, two-way discussion, it is best to signal equality between the participants by, for example, sitting side by side, rather than facing each other; and using 'open' body language, without defensive self-hugging or aggressive gesturing towards the other person.

The purpose of the interview should be clear to all participants. For the interviewer, it is important to use open questions that give the person being interviewed plenty of scope to express their views. Open questions often begin with words such as 'How', 'What', and 'Why'. They invite the speaker to expand on what they have to say. For example, the question 'How would you like your career to develop?' gives more scope to reply than 'Would you like to gain promotion?' Similarly, 'What are your favourite pastimes?' is a better, more open question than 'Do you like swimming?'

The person interviewing may also summarise at various points in order to keep the conversation focused, and to make sure that the person being interviewed is being understood. This is especially important during assessment, counselling or appraisal interviews which serve the purpose of allowing the interviewee to express their thoughts and feelings. A typical summarising statement may begin: 'Let me make sure that I have understood you...'; and may end by a statement such as 'Is that a fair summary?', or 'Do you wish to add anything to that?'

Relaxing the voice

In situations where you feel your voice becoming constricted, try to relax your jaw, shoulders, chest and abdomen. Take a few deep breaths. Breathe in, speak out. Take your time. Breathe in, speak out. And remember to listen.

When speaking with someone who is tense (shown, for example, by a tendency to talk too quickly, or too loudly, or to stumble over words) make a deliberate effort to speak calmly. This will often have the effect of helping the other person to relax.

RECORDING THE VOICE

You may need to record yourself or others in discussions, in order to present evidence for assessment.

Tape recorders often distort the voice, making it sound less vibrant than we expect. You may find that you do not like your own voice on tape. To get the best out of an audio or video recording, use a free-standing microphone and experiment with distance and sound levels until you get a clear recording. This process need take only a minute or so but will improve the sound quality, especially if you wish to submit a recording as evidence of achievement.

Element 2.2 and 3.2: Produce written material

WRITING

Writing is a highly complex activity, at which most people become proficient. It is not just written down speech. Even the dialogue of a stage play or a TV soap opera is only an approximation to everyday speech, with its pauses, hesitations and emphases.

Just as each person's speech is unique, so no two people write exactly alike. Writing is an expression of individuality, as well as an attempt to communicate with other people.

Types of writing

Most professional, everyday writing is *transactional* (i.e., it uses language that is intended to inform or influence other people), and it is this aspect of language that is developed and assessed as a core skill in Communication.

Transactional language can, for the sake of clarity, be sub-divided by purpose into:

Informative = desire to make information available through, e.g. writing records, reports, letters. The information should be true, relevant, reliable and clearly stated.

Instructive/persuasive = desire to influence the

Transactional writing often has strong elements of persuasion.

reader, either through regulation, if the roles of writer and reader carry with them the authority to regulate, and compliance is assumed (e.g. instructions, requests expressed in memos); or through persuasion if the audience is more distant and less controlled by the writer (e.g. advertising, advising, recommending in reports or letters).

Most transactional writing falls into the informative category, but it often has strong elements of persuasion, either directly through what is stated, or indirectly through the words chosen, the layout of the document, etc.

You should be able to write for a variety of purposes, including to give information, to get information, to express or obtain opinions, to exchange ideas and to present an argument.

Audience

When we speak face to face with other people we get rapid feedback because we can see and hear the audience react (even silence is a reaction – and a powerful one). When we write, however, the audience is more distant. For many professional documents the audience may even be people in general (e.g. potential customers). Writing rarely receives immediate feedback, and sometimes feedback is only obtained in a roundabout way (e.g. through sales figures). Because of this lack of immediate feedback when writing, it is important to think of the audience in a more conscious way than we usually do when speaking.

What *role* are you playing as a writer (e.g. expert, friend, adviser)? What role do you expect the audience to play (e.g. general public, informed

expert, friend)? The subject matter of any writing will be expressed differently depending on these roles. For example, many scientific documents are written by experts for experts, and may use complex terms that make the document impossible for non-experts to understand. In contrast, advertisements and many newspaper articles are written so that most people can understand them.

One way to build a sense of audience into your writing is to ask yourself two main questions:

> How well do you know the people for whom you are writing, and how well do they know you?

> How much do you think they will already know about the subject?

You should be able to communicate effectively in writing with a wide variety of people, including people who know you and the subject, and people who neither know you nor about the subject. It is necessary, therefore, to structure what you write to suit the audience.

Planning to write

Remember the three Ws:

> *Why* write (e.g. to inform, persuade, complain)?

> *Who* will read it (e.g. friend, colleague, public)?

> *What* format should it take (e.g. letter, report, memo)?

The process of thinking through these questions will also determine the general style of your writing (e.g. formal, with your own personality concealed, or informal, with your own personality prominent).

It is important to keep your writing *focused* on the nature of the audience and the purpose of the writing. In this way you will be helped to meet the Performance Criteria for PRODUCE WRITTEN MATERIAL.

FORMATS OF WRITING

Different types of written document have conventional formats. Business letters are usually set out in a standard way; formal reports may follow a standard pattern set by an organisation. There is an underlying structure to most formats. It is usual to make clear the subject or purpose of writing towards the beginning; to deal with important points before trivial ones; and to leave conclusions and recommendations until towards the end. This may seem obvious, but inexperienced writers sometimes take a long time to focus and to make plain to the reader what the subject is.

Remember that working people are often very busy. They want documents that are as brief as possible, but that deal clearly with the subject.

Memos

A memo (short for 'memorandum') is an informal note or letter that sets out information as briefly as possible. For convenience, memo outlines are often pre-printed. Here is a typical memo:

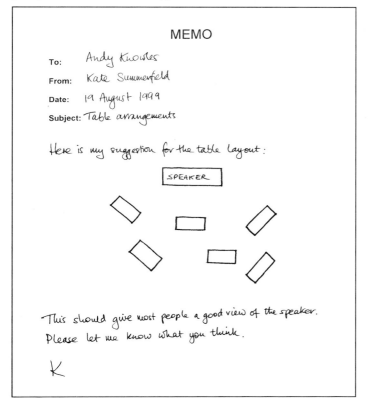

Letters

Letters serve all the possible purposes of written communication and often convey something of the personality of the writer, as well as information about the subject. It is often necessary to choose words with care because *how* a subject is expressed is sometimes as important as *what* is expressed.

Here is a letter of complaint:

> 14 Elm Dr.
> Elmchurch
> EX4 1RK
>
> 24 February 1997
>
> The Planning Officer
> District Council Offices
> 7 Lower George Street
> Dissbury EX9 2JB
>
> Dear Sir/ Madam,
>
> I am writing to object to the proposed building of a road across Green Belt land, between Elmchurch and Brithely. My objections are as follows:
>
> Firstly, I object to even more Green Belt land being lost to tarmac.
>
> Secondly, I do not think that the road is needed. Traffic in the area is heavy, but the present road system is adequate.
>
> Thirdly, I think that the environmental and noise pollution of a new road, so close to peaceful villages, would seriously affect the health and well-being of local people. I am especially worried about the possible harmful effects on the health of our children.
>
> Finally, I think that the huge sum of money that the road would cost would be better spent on providing better public transport, health, education and housing – in other words, on things that will improve the quality of people's lives, instead of blighting them.
>
> Yours faithfully,
>
> *Sandra Townsend*
>
> Sandra Townsend

 STOP AND THINK
How effective do you think this letter is? Is the content relevant? Is it well structured? Is it written in an appropriate style? What does it tell you about the personality of the writer?

Letter writing conventions

People sometimes insist that 'Yours sincerely' goes with the use of a person's name, like 'Dear Mr Napier', whereas 'Yours faithfully' should go after the use of 'Dear Sir' or 'Dear Madam'. These are trivial issues compared to getting the structure of a letter right – e.g. stating clearly in the opening paragraph what the letter is about, using an appropriate tone, and so forth. However, the standard conventions are:

- use a person's name ('Dear Mr Napier') when you know it, and close with 'Yours sincerely';

- use a person's first name ('Dear David') when you know the person quite well, or when writing to a colleague. You may then close with a variety of forms, such as 'Best wishes', instead of, or in addition to 'Yours sincerely';

- if you don't know someone's name but do know their sex, write 'Dear Sir' or 'Dear Madam', and close with 'Yours faithfully';

- if you don't know the sex of the person you are writing to, use an appropriate general term (e.g. 'Dear Customer') and if that is not possible use the rather clumsy 'Dear Sir/Madam';

The best way to familiarise yourself with the conventions of the layout of letters is to look at a few examples from companies and individuals.

Dates

The date is now most often written like this: 14 January 1998, without punctuation or 'th' after the 14. It may be placed below the sender's address, or above the address of the person to whom the letter is being sent.

Changing fashions in punctuating addresses

Taking the example of the address written at the top of a letter or on an envelope, you will find that fashions change in punctuation, and that what would once have been seen as incorrect may in time be regarded as perfectly acceptable:

Miss. G. Smith,	Ms G Smith
'The Larks',	The Larks
47, Cress Rd.,	47 Cress Road
Townley,	Townley
Yorks'.	Yorks YK1 5TN
YK1 5TN	

These changes have come about partly because of the cost of typing all the punctuation which, over a long period, can be very high for a large company (in terms of keying time). However, the changes are also the result of the more relaxed view that, as long as what is written is clearly understandable, it is preferable to aim for simplicity.

As long as what is written is clearly understandable, it is preferable to aim for simplicity.

 STOP AND THINK
What conventions do you use to punctuate addresses and dates? Are you consistent?

Reports

Reports may be set out in any way that makes the contents of the document clear to the reader. It is often appropriate to use sub-headings, and sometimes to indicate sections with numbers or letters.

Very formal reports may be set out using the following sub-headings:

- *Terms of reference*, which state the subject of the report, and whether it includes recommendations. The terms of reference are normally set by whoever commissions the report;

- *The findings*, set out using appropriate sub-headings, numbering and/or lettering;

- *Conclusions*, which summarise the main points of the report;

- *Recommendations*, which may be listed in order of importance.

Most reports follow a less formal structure. The important thing is that the format suits the audience and purpose (PC4) and uses structure and style to present information as clearly as possible (PC5). Remember that some information may be shown most clearly by using appropriate images.

Here are two examples of how reports may be structured.

The assignment report

A report, written as part of a GNVQ assignment, tends to follow a pattern:

- An introductory paragraph states the subject.

- A series of paragraphs, each of which develops the argument or line of reasoning.

Often the main topic of each paragraph will be stated in the opening sentence.

- The argument is supported by evidence (e.g. quotations from books, the presentation of data).

- Images, such as graphs, charts and tables, may be used – either within the report or as appendices – to present information as clearly as possible.

- There will often be a balance of evidence, rather than a one-sided presentation, in order to develop the ideas fully and fairly.

- The final paragraph(s) will summarise the main line of reasoning and draw conclusions.

The purpose of an assignment report is to present information that is relevant and accurate, in a clearly structured, fair and balanced way.

The scientific report

Reports that write up experiments may follow a format like this.

- Title.

- A statement of the hypothesis being tested.

- A statement of the methods used to test the hypothesis.

- Presentation of the results, using tables, graphs, etc., as appropriate.

- Discussion of the findings/conclusions.

- Appendices, giving further details of methods used and results obtained.

Curriculum Vitae (CV)

A Curriculum Vitae or CV (literally, a run through your life) is often requested by employers when inviting applications for a job. It may also be sent out, with an accompanying letter, when enquiring if work is available. It is wise to type a CV.

Most people who read CVs are very busy and they wish to see at a glance whether you may be suited to a particular job. They do not wish to learn everything about your life's history – fascinating as that may be.

There is no right or wrong way to set out a CV, but remember that the visual impact it has may be an important factor in getting an interview. Here is a typical CV:

CURRICULUM VITAE

Paula Davis
37 Knight's Road,
Solihull,
West Midlands,
BM19 9RJ

tel: 0487 366782

AGE: 22

QUALIFICATIONS

St. Thomas More School
GCSEs: English   B
         Maths   C
         Physics   C
         History   A
         French   C

Soulbury College of Further Education
GNVQ
Advanced: Engineering   MERIT

EXPERIENCE

Technician, Brunel Engineering Ltd
At Brunel I am a design technician, working as a member of a small team. I have been abroad several times on projects.

INTERESTS
Dancing, travel, sports

Paula could have added more information, such as the dates of her qualifications and of her employment at Brunel Engineering; brief details of any significant work experience when a student; and the names and addresses of referees.

A typical CV is likely to contain the following order of information:

Name
Address
Telephone number
Age or date of birth
Education, with dates and results

Experience, with dates
Interests
Referees – usually two, with their names, addresses, telephone numbers and, if appropriate, positions.

 STOP AND THINK
Should you experiment with different layouts of your CV and check their impact on friends and tutors?

Information should concentrate on what a prospective employer will need to know; and should emphasise positive achievements.

The accompanying letter

A CV is normally sent with an accompanying letter – typed or handwritten neatly – which should state clearly the job for which you are applying. You may also give brief details of why you are applying and what you are doing at present. The letter should end politely. Here is Paula's letter:

> 37 Knight's Road,
> Solihull,
> West Midlands,
> BM19 9RJ
>
> 14 January, 1998
>
> The Personnel Officer,
> Highbridge Engineering,
> Western Industrial Estate,
> Solihull,
> West Midlands,
> BM6 7QR
>
> Dear Mr Napier,
>
> Senior Design Technician, Ref: AN/471
>
> Thank you for sending me details of this post, for which I now wish to apply. As you will see from the enclosed CV, I am a qualified design technician, with several years experience of design projects with Brunel Engineering.
>
> I am happy at Brunel, but would like to gain experience in another firm and at a more senior level. I think that I am ready to take on more responsibility.
>
> I am available for interview at any time and look forward to hearing from you.
>
> Yours sincerely,
>
> *Paula Davis*
>
> Paula Davis
> Enc. CV

The letter could have been set out differently. For example, the addresses could have been written without punctuation; the paragraphs could have been indented, rather than blocked to the left-hand margin; as could the complimentary close, 'Yours sincerely'. However, these things are not that important. It is important that the letter includes information which is

accurate and relevant (PC1); is legible (PC2); is written following standard conventions of spelling, punctuation and grammar (PC3); and uses structure and style to emphasise meaning (PC5).

Documenting a meeting

Most organisations, whether public or private, hold a variety of meetings that need to be documented, so that people are given notice of what will be discussed; and a record of decisions taken. Company minutes, once they have been agreed and signed as a true record, may be used as legal evidence.

Company Annual General Meetings

A typical notice and agenda for a company Annual General Meeting looks like this:

> **NOTICE OF MEETING**
> Notice is given that the eighth Annual General Meeting of Hudson public limited company will be held at the Roxborough Hotel, Georgetown on Wednesday, 8 June at 11.00 a.m. for the transaction of the following business:
>
> **Ordinary business**
>
> *Resolution 1*
> THAT the accounts and reports of the directors and the auditors for the year ended 31 March 1998 be received.
>
> *Resolution 2*
> THAT the final dividend of 14 pence per share recommended by the directors be declared payable on 16 September 1998 to holders of ordinary shares registered at the close of business on 8 August 1998.
>
> *Resolution 3*
> THAT Mrs R J Hamilton be re-elected as a director of the company.

… and so the notice will continue, sometimes for pages, with accompanying documents, explanatory notes, and forms. Some notices may include agenda items.

However, most meetings are less formal than this, and are likely to follow this sequence:

Calling a meeting

A straightforward notice should be sent well in advance to everyone who may attend. The notice should include all necessary information (PC1); be legible (PC2); be written in conventional English

(PC2); and be set out clearly (PC3). Here is a typical notice for a relatively informal meeting:

> **SWANFIELD COLLEGE**
> The next meeting of the Curriculum Development Committee will take place on Thursday, 16 June at 4.15 p.m. in the Green Room. Please submit items for the agenda, in writing, by Monday 6 June.

Once people have submitted agenda items these will be arranged by the Chair and/or the Secretary of the committee, like this:

> **SWANFIELD COLLEGE**
> The next meeting of the Curriculum Development Committee will take place on Thursday, 16 June at 4.15 p.m.in the Green Room.
>
> AGENDA
> 1) Apologies for absence
> 2) Minutes of the last meeting
> 3) Matters arising
> 4) Items for approval:
>   i   Electronic engineering course
>   ii   Short courses on financial management
>   iii Module on development economics
>
> 5) Items for debate:
>   i   Staff development budget
>   ii   Proposed amendments to assessment system
> 6) Any other business
> 7) Date of next meeting

This is a typical agenda structure for meetings in businesses, schools, colleges and government departments. It deals logically with the business of the meeting:

- Who is present/absent

- Agreement that the record of the last meeting is accurate

- An opportunity to report on any action taken as a result of the last meeting

- A list of the issues to be dealt with, in a particular order

- The opportunity to discuss other issues that people wish to raise

- The arrangements for the next meeting

Under *Matters arising* it is usual to concentrate on finding out if people have carried out what they were asked to do at the last meeting. It is not usual to re-open debates at length.

Under *Any other business* it is not usual to deal with important issues. These should be put on the agenda or tabled for the next meeting. If they are very pressing, however, they may be dealt with immediately, or a special or 'extraordinary' meeting may be called as soon as possible.

Beware agenda manipulation. The person drawing up an agenda can sometimes decide the items for debate. Items left out of an agenda may be more important than those included; and if important items are listed late in an agenda they may be ignored for lack of time.

The minutes

After the meeting, minutes will be drawn up, usually by a committee secretary, but often by a volunteer, or even the Chair. The minutes may look like this:

> **SWANFIELD COLLEGE**
> Minutes of the Curriculum Development Committee held on Thursday, 16 June.
> Present: [the names of everyone at the meeting]
> 1) Apologies for absence: [the names of those who could not attend and who sent their apologies]
> 2) Minutes of the last meeting: the minutes of the last meeting were accepted as a true record.
> 3) Matters arising: Matthew Archer reported that he had booked a speaker to talk about GNVQ at level 5.
> 4) Items for approval:
>   i   Electronic engineering course: approved.
>   ii   Short courses on financial management: approved, subject to meeting an enrolment target of 15 people per course.
>   iii Module on development economics: approved.
> 5) Items for debate:
>   i   Staff development budget: it was agreed that two and a half per cent of budget will normally be given to staff development activities. Budget holders must ensure that they follow this norm and account for spending at the end of each financial year.
>   ii   Proposed amendments to assessment system: it was agreed to set up a feasibility study, chaired by Dr Fraser, to consider the advantages of increased computerisation of assessment in the college. The study is to be submitted to the Committee by December.

> 6)   Any other business: a grant of £200
>   was agreed to Ms Taylor towards
>   conference expenses.
> 7)   Date of next meeting: the next
>   meeting of the Curriculum
>   Development Committee will take
>   place on Thursday, 21 September at
>   4.45 p.m. in the Oval Room.

This is a typical set of minutes from a meeting. Minutes should be as brief as possible, while being accurate and representing fairly what has been discussed. It is particularly important that, if action is to be taken, it is clear what this will be and who will carry it out (e.g. in the next meeting, under *Matters arising*, it will be checked that the task assigned to Dr Fraser has been carried out).

Questionnaire design

If you wish to gather the views of a large number of people, it may be necessary to write a questionnaire. (For a small sample of people, it is often preferable to interview them, using a checklist of questions. This usually yields more detailed information.)

Questionnaire design requires a lot of thought. Questions should be short and straightforward to avoid misinterpretation. To make the results of a questionnaire easier to analyse, it is best to use *closed* questions (i.e. giving respondents a limited range of answers to choose from). However, they do need to allow respondents to express their views accurately, which is not always the case with simple Yes/No choices.

People are often very busy and therefore unable to give a lot of time to answering questionnaires.

Consider the following question:

Did you enjoy sports at school? Yes/No

The suggested response of Yes/No does not give the respondent an opportunity to express in-between feelings (e.g. they quite enjoyed swimming, hated cricket but loved soccer). You could supply a range of answers:

In general, how much did you enjoy sports at school? Very much/a lot/quite a lot/not at all

If you wanted to help people complete the questionnaire quickly, or if you wanted to focus on particular sports, you could give respondents alternatives to choose from, such as:

Please tick the sports you enjoyed at school:

☐   Athletics

☐   Badminton

☐   Basketball

etc.

Another way to gauge a person's opinion or experience more accurately than simply asking for a Yes/No response is to use a scale of letters or numbers, like this:

Please circle the response that most accurately represents your experience: 5 indicates very frequently, 1 indicates never.

I suffer from headaches   1   2   3   4   5

or

I go to the cinema   1   2   3   4   5

You can also obtain an approximation of people's views by giving a few possible responses to a statement. For example:

Please circle the response that is closest to your opinion.

There is too much road traffic in Britain. Agree/ Neutral/ Disagree

However, for some questions you do need a Yes/No response, for example:

Have you ever visited the United States? Yes/No

You may want to give people the option to expand, in which case questions should be *open*, leaving space for respondents to write what they want, for example:

Which sports did you enjoy at school?

is a more open question than, 'Did you enjoy sport at school?'

Questions that begin with words such as, 'how', 'what' or 'why' are often open questions, e.g.:

How do you spend your leisure time?

What were your favourite subjects at school?

Why do you prefer butter to margarine?

Another way to make a questionnaire more open is to ask 'Any Other Comments?'

People are often very busy and therefore unable to give a lot of time to completing questionnaires. Keep them as short as possible.

It is wise to trial or pilot a questionnaire before using it, to discover if any of the questions are difficult to understand or ambiguous; to test general reaction to the length and content of the questionnaire; and to assess how easy it is to interpret and record people's answers.

You may need to begin the questionnaire with some straightforward questions to classify the people who answered it (e.g. name, age, sex). Keep these questions brief, polite and inoffensive. For example, some people may not wish to state their age but may be willing to say in which age band it falls (20–30, 30–40, etc.).

Don't forget to thank people for completing the questionnaire, either on the form itself or personally.

THE STRUCTURE OF WRITING

Paragraphing

Paragraphing is a way of helping the reader to follow what is written. It breaks up the text into more readable sections, and shows how the subject develops from one idea to another. Paragraphs normally contain several sentences but, where the sense demands it, a paragraph may be only one or two sentences long. *I will now change paragraph in order to move on to a new aspect of paragraphing.*

When planning to write, it is sometimes useful to think in terms of paragraphs – giving each main point its own paragraph.

Do you need to leave more white space on the page so as not to overwhelm the reader with writing?

Paragraphs may be separated either by indenting the first line by 1–2 cm, like this one, or by double line spacing between paragraphs, like most of the paragraphs in this book. Unless there is a 'house style', choose whichever you prefer, but be consistent; don't change style within the same document (unless you do it deliberately for effect).

Page layout

Page layout can be very important in helping readers to follow your ideas. It is particularly important when you wish to be very clear or persuasive. Think about:

The length of paragraphs – do you let them wander on for too long?

Indentation – can you enhance clarity by indenting, as I am doing now with these points?

Do you need to leave more white space on the page so as not to overwhelm the reader with writing?

Highlighting

There are a number of ways to highlight and draw attention to key points. **One is to use bold, as here**. Examples of other devices include:

• using asterisks or bullet points

– using dashes

underlining

USING CAPITAL LETTERS

enclosing words in a box

The use of word processors has greatly increased the ease of highlighting parts of documents. However, use these devices with discretion – it is possible to overdo them and make the document more difficult to follow.

STYLE

Style in what you wear is about expressing your personality with flair. In writing too it is possible to express yourself with more or less style through your choice of words and how you structure what you write. Of course, as with clothes, style is a matter of taste and opinion, but it is important, especially at level 3 and above, to think about the style in which you write.

For instance, which of the following sentences do **you** prefer?

> For me work was a new environment, being in school all those years.

or

> After being in school all those years, going to work put me in a new environment.

In my opinion, the style of the second version is better. I think it is clearer.

Here is another example:

> As I lay at my ease, I looked out over the far Southern sea sinking to sleep in the dusk.

Do you think this is stylish?

Personally, I think there are too many sibilants (the repeated 's' sounds) and I find the idea of the 'sea sinking' unhelpful. I think of sinking in the sea, rather than the sea sinking. However, the very next sentence is better:

> The glistening and sparkling of the water passed away – the sea became a great bale of grey-blue silk, soft, smooth, dreamy, like the garment of a sorceress queen.
>
> (Gordon, 1912)

I like the style of this, although I think the sentence could have ended after 'dreamy' – I don't think the last phrase adds to the effectiveness of the sentence. What do you think?

There are no definite 'rules' governing style, but you should consider the impact of your style on the reader. Ask a friend to read your work. Does it have the impact you would like? Is the style appropriate for the audience? For example, the style of a letter applying for a job may be quite different from that of a report for your colleagues of what was decided at a meeting.

Imaginative uses of language

Words – like clothes– can become overused and lose their freshness. Consider words like 'good' and 'nice'. When someone says, 'We had a nice holiday', what are they actually conveying? That the beach was clean and the sea warm? The food was varied and well prepared? They met a lot of friendly people? 'Nice' conveys none of this – it is vague and lacks impact.

 STOP AND THINK
Are there words or expressions that you overuse?

Language may be used in imaginative ways to express information more clearly and forcefully. You may compare one thing with another – 'He's as noisy as a cricket'; 'She is as lithe as a cat'. These are similes. You may use words in ways that are not literally true – 'She is a treasure trove of bright ideas'; 'They left us high and dry'. These are metaphors. Sometimes, like the last example, a metaphor can lose its freshness and power to impress; it becomes clichéd through overuse and loses touch with its literal meaning – in this case the image of a boat stranded by the outgoing tide.

We all use metaphorical language every day. Fiction writers are often particularly skilful at using language in imaginative and fresh ways. Here is an example from Shakespeare's *Hamlet*. Ophelia believes that Hamlet has gone mad. She says, 'Now see that noble and most sovereign reason, like sweet bells jangled, out of tune and harsh.' (Act III. Sc1. 165).

This is an example of an extended metaphor. Here is another example, intended to express information forcefully and memorably:

> Earth is 4,600 million years old. Imagine it as a woman of 46 years We know nothing about the first 7 years of her life. At 42 she began to flower. Dinosaurs appeared when she was 45. Eight months ago mammals appeared. In the middle of last week apes evolved into humanoid creatures. People like us have been around for 4 hours. In

the last hour we have developed agriculture. The Industrial Revolution happened one minute ago.

In the last 60 seconds we have caused the extinction of thousands of species by polluting and destroying rivers, sea, forest and the air.

Will the Earth live to be 47?

We are destroying her; only we can save the Earth.

THE IMPORTANCE OF DRAFTING

A very skilled writer may sometimes finish complex documents in one attempt. However, most people, most of the time, especially if they wish to express complex ideas or opinions with clarity, have to re-draft at least once. Re-drafting is not a sign of weakness as a writer. It shows that thought and practice are needed for most writing beyond the routine.

If you use a word processor it is comparatively easy to re-draft, although many people prefer to use pencil and paper for drafting, and only type their final version. Do whatever you prefer – it is the power of your mind in re-drafting that matters, not the power of your processor.

STOP AND THINK
How often do you re-draft your work?

A very skilled writer may sometimes finish complex documents in one attempt.

THE MECHANICS OF THE ENGLISH LANGUAGE

Who's afraid of grammar?

Grammar is a word that terrifies some people. It refers to the 'rules' or conventions that govern how words are put together to make sense. Many of these conventions are known intuitively by people brought up to speak a language. English speakers simply know that 'The cat sat on the mat' is a grammatically correct sentence, whereas 'Sat the mat the cat on' does not make sense because it is ungrammatical. Each word is correct, but the word order is wrong.

So, grammar is nothing to be afraid of. It simply brings out, in the form of more explicit 'rules' or conventions, what most people know already. You may ask yourself then, why bother with 'rules' if most people already know them?

Sometimes, because people ignore the 'rules', they do not make themselves clear. Pointing this out can help avoid similar problems in future. For example, the sentence 'The student stroked a cat <u>in a blue shirt</u>' breaks the 'rule' of grammar that words that belong together should be placed together. The sentence should be written: 'The student <u>in a blue shirt</u> stroked the cat.' This is a light-hearted example (and jokes often depend on bending the normal rules of language). Bear in mind, however, that lawyers make a living out of sentences that are ambiguous and open to interpretation.

A word of warning
The structures of all languages are very complex and change over time. The word 'rules' is in inverted

commas to show that the rules are not inflexible, absolute rules but conventions or guides to what should happen most of the time. This is why in Performance Criteria 3 for ELEMENT 2: PRODUCE WRITTEN MATERIAL, you are required to use grammar that follows *standard conventions*, not rules.

Different dialects of any language, including English, have different grammatical conventions. For instance:

'I ain't never seen him.'

'I done it.'

'Stupid you ain't.'

are all grammatical in *non-standard* English. In *standard* English, for the core skill of Communication (i.e. the English that is most closely associated with education, the professions and formal documents) the sentences would be written:

'I have never seen him.'

'I did it.'

'You are not stupid.'

When speaking it is often acceptable (or even expected) that we will use non-standard forms of grammar, whereas when writing for professional purposes it is usually expected that we will use standard English grammar. However, even the grammar conventions of standard English change with time. For example, the word 'data' is plural, and therefore should take a plural verb (e.g. 'The data are clear'). But in fact it is now acceptable to break the 'rule' and to write, 'The data is clear'.

Language is always changing

Language is ever-changing because human beings are ever-changing. Dynamic societies, such as those of the English-speaking world today, give rise to many new words and language conventions.

To illustrate the way that words change, consider that the word 'glamour' has its origins in the word 'grammar'. 'Grammar' originally referred to writing and the letters of the alphabet. The word gradually developed to refer to learning itself (from which derived 'grammar school'). From 'grammar', meaning learning, developed 'grammar', meaning occult learning or magic. Eventually this changed slightly to 'glamour', which in turn began a process of development as a word in its own right. Today the meaning of 'glamour' as magic has been forgotten

It may help you to be able to identify and name these elements of sentences, but this is not essential for their effective use.

but you can still sense this older meaning if you think of glamour as 'bewitching beauty'.

Word classes

Words may be classified, according to their use in sentences, into:

Nouns: car, job, justice, France

Pronouns: it, he, who

Adjectives: large, interesting, green

Verbs: run, speak, think

Adverbs: slowly, positively, happily

Prepositions: over, under, on

Conjunctions: and, but, because

Interjections: damn, blimey

It is important to remember that you speak and write using these parts of speech all the time. It may help you to be able to identify and name these elements of sentences, but this is not essential for their effective use.

Sentence structure

A sentence is a group of words that makes sense without the need to add further words. For instance,

'The sat on the mat' is not a sentence, 'The cat sat on the mat' is.

Keep control of the length of sentences. Don't let them ramble on so that the meaning gets lost. Get a friend to check your work for clarity. Most of all, *make sure that your sentences make sense.*

Sentences come in many sizes and shapes, but they all share the same basic characteristics, because of their function. Most sentences contain three elements : subject, verb and object e.g.:

I (subject) like (verb) it (object)

Sentences do not always have an object – The child laughs. Time flies. – are sentences.

Sometimes, part of a sentence is 'understood'. Thus 'Like it!' can be a sentence because the subject 'I' is *understood*. Similarly, if you look again at the second paragraph of this section, one sentence reads: 'Keep control of the length of sentences.' 'Keep control' is the verb; 'of the length of sentences' is the object. The subject is 'You', but this is *understood*. However, if I had written 'You of the length of sentences', it would not be a sentence, because it doesn't make sense without the missing element – the verb. Most sentences are built around verbs, and it is this element that is sometimes missed by people who have difficulty with writing.

It is not always easy to recognise the elements of a sentence, but you can tell when an essential element is missing because the words do not make sense together. However, you do not have to unpick sentences to see how they are made up, any more than you need to take a car apart in order to be able to drive it. And unpicking sentences can be tricky. For example, sometimes the subject may be mysterious. In 'It is raining in Glasgow', what is 'It'? Similarly, an object can be mysterious, as in '(You) Watch it!' Again, what is 'it'? None the less, you can see that these are sentences because all three elements – subject, verb and object are there. Even the single word 'Enough!' can be a sentence if it is clear from what has been written before what the object is. If , for instance, the subject is 'I', in its full form, the sentence would read 'I have had enough of (whatever it is)'. Similarly, 'No' can be a sentence.

Word order

The order of words in a sentence can affect the meaning. 'The student stroked the cat in a blue shirt'

has already been given as an example. Another is, 'The car needs servicing badly', when what was meant was 'The car badly needs servicing'. In everyday speech these ambiguities in meaning often do not matter, because it is quite clear what is actually meant. However, in writing, especially for an unknown audience, it is important to get the word order right, so that there is no room for doubt about the meaning.

Verbs

Verbs are the words around which most sentences are structured. Verbs have been called 'doing words', because most of them are about doing something (e.g. run, write, smile, think). However, some verbs are not about doing, but about a state of affairs (e.g. 'it is easy'; 'I have had enough'; 'I am here'). The important thing to remember is that nearly all sentences should have at least one verb.

Verbs change according to who or what their subject is. Take the verb 'like'. Depending on who is doing the liking, it is written (the technical term is 'conjugated') like this:

I like

You like

S/he likes

We like

You (plural) like

They like

Most verbs in the present tense add an 's' in the third person singular (i.e. when the verb refers to she or he or it). Other examples are: I smile – she smiles; you talk – he talks; we grow – it grows.

By listening to people using language, children absorb the structures used. In most cases this leads to them using sentence structures that are grammatically correct, because most people, most of the time use these structures without the need for conscious thought. However, if a person absorbs speech habits that are not grammatically correct in standard English then these may easily become a fixed habit. In some non-standard uses of English people may say, 'She smile', rather than 'She smiles', or 'He talk', rather than 'He talks'. While in everyday speech this may be perfectly acceptable (or even expected), in writing, especially for professional purposes, it is necessary to use standard English grammar.

Verbs also change with *tense*, depending on, for example, whether they refer to present, past or future events. Thus:

> I like (present); I liked (past); I will like (future)

In the past and future tenses the form of the verb does *not* change with person:

> I liked   I will like
>
>   He liked   She will like

Active and passive sentences

'Nurses look after patients' is an active sentence; whereas 'Patients are looked after by nurses' is a passive sentence. If you wish your writing to sound direct and forceful it is preferable to use active sentences – they tend to be shorter and clearer. Passive sentences are sometimes preferred in formal documents because they sound weightier. Here are some other examples of the difference between active and passive sentence constructions:

> The trainee designed the logo. (active)
>
> The logo was designed by the trainee. (passive)
>
> The wheel was turned by the engineer. (passive)
>
> The engineer turned the wheel. (active)

Switching tense

Sometimes writers change tense without meaning to, and switch from past to future or present in ways they do not intend and that confuse the reader:

> I looked (*past*) in the window. I open (*present*) the door. I saw (*past*) a man I recognised (*past*).

Here the reader is being given an account of an event in the past and the use of the present tense ('I open') is confusing.

If the writer deliberately decides to use the present tense to describe an event in the past, in order to make it more immediate, it can be very effective:

> I look in the window. I open the door. I see a man I recognise.

Here *every* verb is in the present tense. The important thing is to be in control of your writing, and not to switch tenses in ways that may blur your intended meaning.

Agreement

A common mistake is to break the agreement rule (i.e. that the verb should 'agree' with the subject) and to say, for instance, 'We <u>was</u> disappointed with the result', or 'We <u>was</u> happy'. This may sound perfectly acceptable when speaking informally. However, when speaking in an interview, or when writing, it is more appropriate to stick to the rule that noun and verb agree – 'We <u>were</u> disappointed with the result'; 'We <u>were</u> happy'.

There are some words (e.g. 'family', 'class') that can be regarded as either plural or singular. Thus it is correct to write either: 'My family is coming', or 'My family are coming'; 'The class is going', or 'The class are going'.

Split infinitives

The infinitive of a verb is its basic form – 'to win', 'to go', 'to climb'. Putting words between 'to' and the verb can sometimes sound awkward: 'It is wise to in advance do some preparation' sounds clumsy compared to 'It is wise to do some preparation in advance'; whereas 'To boldly go where no one has gone before' may be a perfectly acceptable split infinitive. This is a matter of opinion and personal preference about which you should be aware.

Of or have?

The verb 'have', in for example, 'I should have known better' is sometimes pronounced 'of'. This has led to some writers writing 'of' instead of 'have', even though there is no verb 'to of'. It is grammatically correct to use 'have'.

Nouns and pronouns

A noun is a word that names (e.g. refers to a thing or abstract idea, person, or place). Examples of nouns are:

> names of objects, big or small (car, book, mouse, sky)
>
> words that refer to ideas (justice, mercy, freedom)
>
> names of people and places (London, Joanne, Paris, Matthew)

words that refer to knowledge (philosophy, plumbing, communication)

Nouns are often preceded by an article ('a' or 'the'), although some abstract nouns (e.g. 'justice') may stand alone.

Most sentences have nouns in them, or the nouns are understood, as in 'Stop it!' where the noun (e.g. 'John, stop it!') is clear from the context.

It can be repetitious to use nouns all the time, so we often substitute pronouns for them. An example is, 'When Mr Davis came into the room he was warmly welcomed', which sounds less clumsy than 'When Mr Davis came into the room Mr Davis was warmly welcomed'. Examples of pronouns are: 'he', 'she', 'it', 'they', 'their'. When using pronouns, you must make sure that it is clear to which nouns they refer. Read over your work, or get a friend to check it, to ensure that you have achieved clarity.

These, those and them

'These' and 'those' are examples of demonstrative pronouns, used to point out something. If what is pointed out is near, 'these' is used e.g. 'These apples are juicy'. If what is pointed out is farther off, 'those' is used e.g. 'Those hill in the distance'.

Avoid using the personal pronoun 'them' when 'these' or 'those' should be used. Sentences such as 'Them apples are juicy'; 'Them hills in the distance' are ungrammatical.

I or me?

Should you write:

'Mia and **I** went to the pictures', or 'Mia and **me** went to the pictures'?

'Joanne looked at Mia and **I**', or 'Joanne looked at Mia and **me**'?

The 'rule' is that if the pronoun ('I' or 'me') is the subject of a sentence, 'I' should be used; if it is the object of the sentence, 'me' should be used. In the first example 'Mia and I' is the subject and so 'I' is correct. Another way of thinking about it is that, without Mia, the sentence would be 'I went to the pictures'. This sounds right. Adding Mia does not change anything.

STOP AND THINK!
Which of the sentences in the second example is correct? Take out the words 'Mia and'. Which of the remaining sentences sounds correct? 'Joanne looked at I' or 'Joanne looked at me'?

The correct sentence is 'Joanne looked at Mia and me', because 'Mia and me' is the object of the sentence, therefore, 'me', rather than 'I', is correct.

Adjectives and adverbs

You can add adjectives and adverbs to sentences to tell the reader more about the subject, the object or the verb. The sentence:

The man (subject) likes (verb) ice-cream (object)

can be extended by, for example, adding:

an adjective to the subject: The *smart* man

an adverb to the verb: *really* likes

an adjective to the object: *vanilla* ice-cream

creating the sentence:

The smart man really likes vanilla ice-cream.

Comparative adjectives

'More simple' or 'simpler'? Sometimes people find it difficult to decide which is preferable. What do you think?

Very often it sounds more harmonious to use the shorter construction. 'The text was simpler than she expected' sounds better than 'The text was more simple than she expected'. So you have:

simple	simpler	simplest
cool	cooler	coolest

However, some comparisons need to use the word 'more' (e.g. 'She is more beautiful than her sister', rather than 'She is beautifuler than her sister') so you have:

beautiful	more beautiful	most beautiful
satisfied	more satisfied	most satisfied

Positions of prepositions

The last sentence in the paragraph on split infinitives could have been written, 'This is a matter of opinion and personal preference that you should be aware of.' But there has long been a 'rule' in English that a sentence should not end with a preposition (words such as: on, by, for, through, with, of).

Once again this is a matter of opinion and personal preference. Winston Churchill, British Prime Minister during the Second World War, made fun of the 'rule' by showing how convoluted a sentence can become if you try to apply it. Instead of writing the direct and harmonious sentence, 'This is something I will not put up with', he wrote, 'This is something up with which I will not put.'

Who or whom?

In very formal English usage, 'whom' rather than 'who' is used after a preposition, or when it forms the object rather than the subject of a sentence. So, for example, 'Our leader, in whom we believe' (after preposition); 'He is the man who did it' ('He' is the subject of the sentence) but 'He is the man whom I met yesterday' ('I' is the subject and 'He' is the object of the sentence).

However, this 'rule' is disappearing from everyday use and, if applied, can sometimes sound clumsy or even faintly ridiculous. Most people would now say, 'He is the man who I met yesterday'. People would also probably break two 'rules' (who/whom *and* preposition) and say, 'Our leader, who we believe in'.

That, who, which and what

Relative pronouns, such as 'that', 'who', and 'which', are used to begin relative clauses (a clause is a group of words in a sentence with their own subject and verb).

There are two kinds of relative clauses.

Some clauses explain something in the main part of the sentence, without which the sentence would not make complete sense. These begin with 'that', e.g:

This is the song *that* John Lennon wrote.

She is the best singer *that* I have ever heard.

Sometimes, as in these examples, it is possible to drop the word 'that' without altering the meaning.

The second kind of relative clause gives additional information in a sentence that already makes sense. These begin with 'who' ('whom') or 'which', e.g.:

Julie Tullis, *who* climbed K2, was a brave woman.

Here, the main sentence 'Julie Tullis was a brave woman' could make sense on its own, 'who climbed K2' gives additional information. Here is another example:

I gave him £10, *which* was all I could afford.

Notice that 'that' may refer to people or things (song or singer), whereas 'who' usually refers to people (Julie Tullis) and 'which usually refers to things (£10).

The relative pronoun 'what' is sometimes used in non-standard English instead of 'who' (e.g. 'It's the rich what gets the fun; it's the poor what gets the blame'; 'He's the bloke what done it'). However, in standard English the pronoun 'who' should be used.

Less or fewer?

There is often confusion about whether you should write 'less' or 'fewer' in a sentence such as, 'There are less/fewer cars on the road'. The convention is that if a number of objects is being referred to, rather than an amount, use 'fewer'. So it should be 'There are fewer cars on the road'.

However, you would say, 'He takes less milk on cornflakes', not 'He takes fewer milk on cornflakes', because you have an amount of milk, rather than individual bits of milk.

Gender

Referring to both men and women when writing the sentence 'Each person should remain seated at. . . desk', should you write 'his', 'her', 'his/her', or 'their' desk? When 'his' is used, it is claimed that women are somehow included, in the same way as they are assumed to be included in the word 'man'

Research has shown that the use of the word 'man' implies that women are excluded.

when it is used to refer to human beings in general. But research has shown that this is not the case and that it implies that women are excluded; people tend to think only of *men* when 'man' is used (e.g. 'the man in the street', 'man-made'). Repeated use of 'his/her' is clumsy, so it is acceptable to write 'their desk', even though 'their', being plural, would normally take a plural noun, 'desks'.

DOUBLE NEGATIVES

In some non-standard English dialects it is acceptable to say sentences such as:

> I didn't say nothing.

which contain two negatives that, in a sense, cancel one another out. Literally, this sentence means 'I said something'. In fact the context, or occasion when it is used, and the tone of voice can make plain what is meant. However, when writing for professional purposes this would be seen as ungrammatical. In standard English it should read: 'I said nothing', or 'I didn't say anything'.

PUNCTUATION

Punctuation has two main purposes:

> to enable written language to be read in a way that increases the reader's understanding;
>
> to give an indication of the sounds of speech.

The meaning of spoken words is made clear in a number of ways (e.g. loudness, pitch, speed, etc.). Think what different meanings the simple words, 'Open the door' can convey depending on how they are spoken (e.g. they could imply 'I have a present for you'; 'I'm fed up standing here'; 'This is the Police'). In writing it is necessary to punctuate in order to convey some of these possible meanings (e.g. 'Open the door?', or 'Open the door!')

Capital letters

Capitals may be used to emphasise text. It is a matter of personal choice whether you choose to emphasise writing in this way. For example, because PUNCTUATION is a new and important section of this guide, it has been emphasised by the use of capital letters.

Capital letters are also used in the following ways:

- First letter of a sentence

- The personal pronoun, 'I'

- Beginning of direct speech – she said, 'Hello.'

- First letter of a proper noun, such as:

  days of the week – Sunday, Monday
  months of the year – December, January
  people's names – Mia, Hannah, Matthew
  place names – Oxford, New York
  titles of books, films, etc. – *Jaws, Red Dwarf*

- Titles of people or organisations – the Prime Minister, the Queen, the National Society for the Prevention of Cruelty to Children (NSPCC)

- People's initials – J.R.R. Tolkien

- Abbreviations – NSPCC, NCVQ, BBC, AA

Full stops

Full stops mark the end of sentences, unless another mark (! ?) is used instead. Without the use of full stops it might be difficult to follow the meaning of what is written, e.g

> Jesse Boot sold medicines cheaply in 1892 he began to make drugs by 1900 he had 126 shops

STOP AND THINK
Where could you put a full stop to clarify the meaning?
Answer: **Jesse Boot sold medicines cheaply. In 1892 he began to make drugs. By 1900 he had 126 shops.**

The comma

Commas help to make sentences easier to read and clearer, by separating them into parts (clauses, phrases, lists). Consider the sentence:

> Peter a psychiatrist believes that handled well organised activities can help a child.

The meaning of this sentence can be clarified by adding commas.

STOP AND THINK
Where would you add commas?
The basic sentence is, 'Peter believes that organised activities can help a child.' The other parts of the sentence are additions that provide further information. They can be marked off from the basic part by commas, 'Peter, a psychiatrist, believes that, handled well, organised activities can help a child.'
In this way the sentence becomes easier to read and to understand.

Semi-colons and colons

A full stop brings a sentence to a halt; a comma produces a pause; a semi-colon can be thought of as half way between, producing a longer pause than a comma. It is used, like the comma, to help the reader understand the structure of the sentence. Consider this lengthy sentence:

> Matthew described what he carried in his pocket: 'A whistle, in case I meet a wolf; a clip, in case I meet a crocodile; and a small, plastic zebra, in case I wish to cross a road.'

Here you can see how the use of commas and semi-colons helps to break up the sentence and emphasise its meaning. In the sentence a colon is used to introduce Matthew's list. It is also used at the end of the sentence before to introduce the example.

Here is another example of the use of colons to introduce a list, and semi-colons to separate the different parts:

> 'Even fairy-stories as a whole have three faces: the Mystical towards the Supernatural; the Magical towards Nature; and the Mirror of scorn and pity towards Man.'
>
> (Tolkien, 1975)

Inverted commas

In the examples above, inverted commas have been used to show that the words were spoken or written by someone other than the writer of this book. In the first example Matthew spoke the words about what was in his pocket; in the second example the words were written by J.R.R. Tolkien in a book called *Tree and Leaf.*

All the actual words spoken or written should be inside the inverted commas, but if these words are interrupted by, for example, *he said*, these words are not direct speech (i.e. they are not what someone actually said, but are an explanation or commentary about who said the words). For example:

> The doctor looked concerned (commentary), 'Please take three of these tablets,' (direct speech) he said (commentary), 'and drink plenty of water.' (direct speech)

Notice that each sentence of direct speech begins as all sentences should, with a capital letter, and the punctuation of the direct speech is inside the inverted commas. In other words, punctuate what is said in the normal way. If you interrupt what is actually said by words such as *he said; she asked*, then these words should be suitably punctuated, for example:

> 'What are these tablets called?', she asked, 'They're big enough to be Flying Saucers.'

The best place to see the use of inverted commas for direct speech is in novels, although a few novelists dispense with inverted commas altogether, preferring to show speech by other means. Here is an example from James Joyce's *Portrait of the Artist*:

> The fellows talked together in little groups.
>
> One fellow said:
>
> – They were caught near the Hill of Lyons.
>
> (Joyce, 1916)

Here, Joyce has introduced the direct speech by a colon followed, on the next line, by a dash. However, it is still clear what is commentary and what is actual direct speech.

Another point to note about writing direct speech is that the convention is to start a new paragraph each time the speaker changes.

Inverted commas can also be used to show that the meaning of a word is vague or debatable. For example, in the sentence, *The 'effective' manager treats staff with respect*, the word 'effective' is in inverted commas to show that it may mean one or more of a number of things, such as well liked, efficient, free from stress, etc.

Reported speech

Sometimes it is preferable to report what has been spoken, rather than to write it out word for word in direct speech.

 STOP AND THINK
Look at the example of the doctor and patient above. If you get rid of the inverted commas and report what has been said, what would you write or say?

Here is a possible report of what was spoken:

> The doctor looked concerned. He asked the patient to take three tablets and to drink lots of water. She looked in alarm at the large, round tablets and asked if they were called Flying Saucers.

If you take the minutes of meetings it can be very tedious to write down people's actual words. It is usually advisable to report what they have said, summarising only important statements and decisions.

Hyphens

A hyphen is a sign (-) used to join the parts of a compound word (e.g. 'forget-me-not'). Some words (e.g. 'headmaster') have become one word after a period of being hyphenated (head-master).

Hyphens should be distinguished from dashes – which are longer and may be used instead of commas (as here) or brackets.

Brackets

Brackets are signs – ( ) { } [ ] – used in pairs to mark off examples (or other additional material) from the main part of a sentence.

Material within brackets should be punctuated normally. The next section, on *Inverted commas* has a number of examples of the use of brackets.

? Question marks?

When speaking, it is usually plain that a question is being asked because the pitch of speech changes. Even a single word like 'Hello' can be an exclamation, a question or a grumble, depending on how it is said.

When writing, it is necessary to give the reader extra clues about what the spoken words actually mean. The reader can tell if, 'The tablets will do her good' is a question or a statement by whether or not it is followed by a question mark.

! Exclamation marks!

The last example could also be written, 'The tablets will do her good!' This has the effect of conveying in writing what would be shown in actual speech by, for example, loudness of voice, rising pitch of voice, and facial expression. It gives the reader a clue to the actual impact and meaning of the words. However, take care not to over-use exclamation marks – if used too much they can give an impression of hysteria.

Apostrophe

One of the most tricky punctuation marks for people to use is the apostrophe. It is used in two ways:

- to show that letters or numbers have been omitted (e.g. it's = it is; can't = can not; don't = do not)

- to show possession (e.g. Mia's jumper; Frank's piano)

However, some words can cause confusion. In 'Its safe to open its cage', which 'its' takes an apostrophe?

The answer is the first, because it is short for 'It is', whereas the second is a word like 'hers', 'ours', 'yours', 'theirs', 'whose', all of which show possession, without need for apostrophes. So if you can substitute 'it is' for 'its', you need to use an apostrophe.

'Susan's gone', and 'Susan's boyfriend' are examples of the use of apostrophe to show omission (Susan has gone) and possession (the boyfriend of Susan).

You can also use an apostrophe if you want to leave some numbers out of a year (e.g. '68 for 1968), but it must be clear what century you are writing about.

The possessive apostrophe and words ending in 's'

Singular nouns add an 's' after the apostrophe – 'Brad's pen'; 'the lion's cage'. This is still true for singular nouns that already end in 's' – the walrus's whiskers. Plural nouns that end in 's' (as most plural nouns do) take the apostrophe alone and do not add a second 's' – 'the Liberals' policies'; 'the lions' cages'. Plural nouns that do not end in 's' follow the normal rule – 'children's shoes'; 'women's issues'. In *every* case, the apostrophe is immediately after what or who is the possessor.

Abbreviations

Abbreviations usually have a full stop after them to show that they have been cut short, for example:

approx.   etc.   Insp.

However, some abbreviations do not need full stops:

- Contractions (where the middle of the word is omitted and the last letter is retained, such as: Mr, Mrs, Ms, Rd, St, Ave, Dr)

- Capital letters (MP, AA, NCVQ, BBC, UN, EU)

- Acronyms (pronounceable abbreviations, such as NATO, GATT)

- Measurements and quantities (mm, g, p [= pence])

The 'rules' of abbreviation, and punctuation in general, are becoming more relaxed.

SPELLING

Many people worry about the standard of their spelling. Most people make errors from time to time. Darwin, for example, in the log of his journey on the *Beagle* spelt 'yacht' as 'yatch', and 'broad' as 'broard'. Spelling English is more difficult than, for example, spelling Spanish. This is because there is not a regular correspondence between the way words sound when spoken, and the way they look on the page when written. 'To', 'two' and 'too' all sound alike; 'plough' and 'rough' have the same ending but are pronounced differently.

Learning to spell correctly is a matter of practice. The more you read and write, the more proficient you will become. However, there are some 'rules' that you can learn to help you, and it is possible, and a good idea, to memorise or keep a note of words that you misspell frequently.

Make use of a good-quality dictionary. This will give you information about the pronunciation of words and which part of speech a word forms (e.g. verb, noun, etc.) as well as the correct spelling. It is usual to look up the 'head word' (or 'root'). For example, if you are uncertain about how to spell 'beginning', then look up 'begin' and you will find words built on this root, including 'beginning'.

United Kingdom Acronym society, May I help you?

UKAS

Word-processing programs also have spell checks that you can use to improve your work. However, these are no substitute for being able to spell correctly.

A list of words that are frequently misspelled

! STOP AND THINK
Here are some words that may cause difficulty. Ask someone to test you on them. Highlight those you cannot spell correctly and try to learn them. Keep a list of other words that you find difficult to spell.

accelerate	counsellor	professional
accessible	(adviser)	psychological
accommodate	credible	questionnaire
adviser *but*	disappear	queue
advisory	embarrass	representative
aesthetic	exaggerate	responsible
barbecue	familiar	success
beggar	fulfil	sufficient
beginning	gauge	transmit
benefited	literature	vinegar
camera	maintenance	visible
commit	moustache	
committee	necessary	
councillor	occasion	
(member of a	parallel	
council)	possess	

'Rules' of spelling

There are some 'rules' you can try to follow in order to improve your spelling. However, there is no substitute for practising – reading and writing.

Forming plurals
The rule is add 's'. However, there are a number of exceptions:

words ending in 's', 'x', 'z', 'ch', 'sh' take 'es' – pass/passes; push/pushes

words ending in 'o' take 'es' – potato/potatoes

words ending in 'y' become 'ies' – lady/ladies

words ending in 'f', or 'fe' replace 'f' with 'v' and add 's' – knife/knives (there are some exceptions to this – roof/roofs; belief/beliefs; dwarf/dwarfs)

Some words still use their Latin or Greek endings in the plural:

words ending in 'is' become 'es' – thesis/theses; crisis/crises; axis/axes

words ending in 'a' become 'ae' – formula/formulae; penumbra/penumbrae (however, it is becoming more usual to use 'formulas' and 'penumbras').

Of course, some English words are eccentric and follow no rule (e.g. child/children; mouse/mice). This is why it is necessary to become used to writing words – learning rules may not always be of help.

Other 'rules'

The most well known rule of English spelling is that you put 'i' before 'e' except after 'c' (e.g. 'chief', 'friend'). However, there are a number of exceptions (e.g. 'weird', 'seize', 'weir').

Sometimes, 'ce' and 'se' endings are confused (e.g. advice/advise). The rule is that most 'ce' endings are of nouns – 'the advice'; 'se' endings are of verbs – 'to advise'. Similarly, 'the practice/to practise'; 'the licence/to license'.

Often, people get confused with some verb endings – is it 'compelled' or 'compeled'? 'Benefited' or 'benefitted'?

The rule is that if the root word ('compel', 'benefit') has more than one syllable, and the stress is on the last syllable then you double the consonant. So 'compel', because it is a word of more than one syllable, with the stress on the last syllable, doubles the last letter to become 'compelled'. The word 'benefit', on the other hand, has the stress on the first, not the last syllable, so the final letter, 't', is not doubled and the word becomes 'benefited'.

Words that are sometimes confused

Some words cause difficulty because they are similar to other words of different meaning. For example:

accept/except (I accept the invitation; everyone will go, except Jack)

It is only through using such words a number of times in your writing that you will feel comfortable with them. If you have any difficulty with the words in the list below, write a few sentences in which you try to use them correctly. Get a friend to check over your work. Here are some more examples of sentences that could be written to practise using these words:

We accept credit cards.

All the children, except Tom, won a prize.

You can also practise words that are based on 'accept/except':

The Oscar acceptance speech was witty.

She took exception to the way he talked to her.

Try these:

affect/effect ('I felt the effect'; 'The new rules will not affect me')

aloud/allowed ('Please read aloud'; 'Smoking is not allowed')

chose/choose ('I chose a red dress' [past tense]; 'I choose you' [present tense])

continual/continuous ('Drip, drip, drip – the leak was continual'; 'There was a continuous flow of water from the broken pipe')

current/currant ('I floated with the current'; 'She ate a currant bun')

dependant/dependent ('My baby is my dependant'; 'Whether we go is dependent on having enough money')

lay/lie ('The dog lay in its basket'; 'Alison said that she would never lie')

Loose/lose ('The tooth was loose'; 'He didn't want to lose it') new/knew ('The house is new'; 'I knew it all along')

passed/past ('I passed the pub on my way to work'; 'In the past [time] people walked faster'; 'I walked past [position] the pub on my way to work')

practice/practise ('The doctor's practice was busy'; 'Sam practised the piano')

principle/principal ('I object to bullying on principle'; 'the College Principal was a fair woman')

quiet/quite ('The boy was very quiet'; 'He did not know quite what to do')

stationary/stationery ('The train was stationary'; 'I took out some stationery to write a letter')

their/they're/there ('Their coats are hanging up'; 'They're [they are] very heavy'; 'You will find them over there')

to/too ('I am going to Florence'; 'Rebecca is coming too' [i.e. also]; 'He is too eager' [i.e. excessively])

threw/through ('Sam threw the ball for the dog'; 'I can see through you')

were/we're ('We were happy'; 'We're [we are] happy')

who's/whose ('Who's [who is] going to the party?'; 'Whose coat is this?')

your/you're ('Your mother is here'; 'You're [you are] beautiful')

Element 2.3 and 3.3: Use images

Confucius is supposed to have said that 'a picture is worth a thousand words'. Communication is dominated by images – cinema, television, advertising, magazines, and newspapers all make heavy use of images, to the extent that, sometimes, words become secondary or even redundant.

It is often very helpful when writing and speaking to use images to illustrate points that you wish to make. When you do, it is important that the images are in fact relevant to what you say or write, and are not merely padding – PC 1; that they are suited to the audience (e.g. how much will they know about the subject?), the situation (e.g. is it an informal discussion or a formal presentation?) and the purpose of the communication (e.g. to entertain, persuade, convey ideas accurately?) – PC2; and that they illustrate clearly the points being made (e.g. by being used at an appropriate place in a document or time in a presentation) – PC3.

What sorts of images can I use?

All sorts of images may be used to support writing or speaking. There is no limit to the type of image that may be used, other than that it must satisfy the Performance Criteria for USING IMAGES. Most images are two dimensional (e.g. maps, sketches, pictures) but you may use three dimensional models (e.g. a scale model of a product or building).

You are expected to be able to select suitable images (e.g. from material you have read) and to produce your own images, by hand or using a computer, in order to illustrate points that you make in speaking and in writing.

Do you have to be very skilful to use images?

The answer is no. Most people can use images without any problem at all. Schools, colleges and workplaces have all sorts of images readily available: in newspapers, journals, books, and libraries.

If you can't find an appropriate image, it is not difficult to take a photograph; draw a diagram, table or chart; or even to draw a sketch.

 STOP AND THINK
Do you make sufficient use of images to support your speaking and writing? Do you need to experiment with using a wider variety of images?

EXAMPLES OF IMAGES

The names given to particular kinds of image are sometimes interchangeable. Some charts may be called diagrams, some sketches may be called maps, some tables may be called charts. Do not worry about what you call an image, as long as its use helps you to communicate more effectively.

Sketching

Sketching does not require fine artistic skills – even matchstick people can be used to good effect to illustrate or explain a point.

Symbols

A symbol is a mark or conventional sign representing a quality or an idea. We are surrounded by symbols, some of which we scarcely notice as symbols – a lion may represent power and pride; the cross represents Christianity. Symbols can be powerful images. They are often used by advertisers, and in propaganda – think of the registered trademark symbol, the Union Jack, or the Nazi swastika. Here are some examples of symbols:

Do you know what they all mean?

Logos

A logo is an image used as the badge or symbol of an organisation. It should be eye-catching and memorable, because the purpose is to make people more aware of the organisation. Do you recognise these logos?

Panda device © 1986 WWF – World Wide Fund For Nature (formerly World Wildlife Fund)

Diagrams

A diagram is a sketch that shows the main features of a particular object or process. Like many other types of image it is not an accurate portrayal of the object or process, but a simplified image that conveys the main features for the purpose of clear illustration. For example:

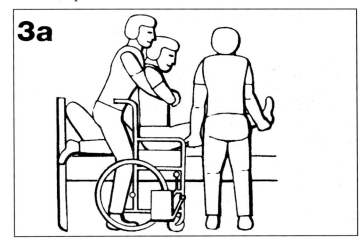

How to lift someone safely

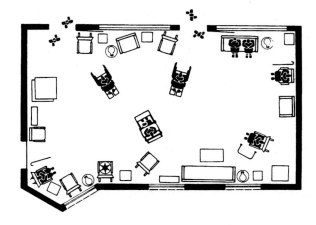

The layout of a building

Charts

There are many types of charts – for example, navigational charts; graphs; sheets of tabulated information. They present information in a 'see-at-a-glance' form.

A temperature chart enables doctors and nurses to see how a patient is progressing over time.

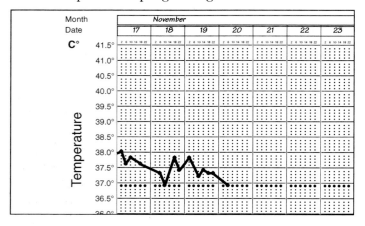

A music chart shows what music is popular at a particular time.

TOP 40 ALBUMS

THIS WEEK	HIGHEST	WEEKS ON			
1	1	1	CROSS ROAD – THE BEST OF ....BON JOVI (Jambco)	
2	1	3	MONSTER...R.E.M. (Warner Brothers)	★
3	3	1	DOG MAN STAR ....SUEDE (Nude)	
4	2	2	NO NEED TO ARGUE ....THE CRANBERRIES (Island)	●
5	3	2	THE HIT LIST ....CLIFF RICHARD (EMI)	●
6	2	8	TWELVE DEADLY CYNS ... AND THEN SOME.......................	●
			....CYNDI LAUPER (Epic)	●
7	1	7	THE THREE TENORS IN CONCERT 1994...............................	
			............CARRERAS/DOMINGO/PAVAROTTI (Teldec)	★
8	8	1	MOVE IT! ....REEL 2 REAL (Positive)	○
9	1	4	SONGS.................................LUTHER VANDROSS (Epic)	●
10	1	59	MUSIC BOX ....MARIAH CAREY (Columbia)	★4
11	1	25	PARKLIFE...BLUR (Food)	★
12	1	7	DEFINITELY MAYBE ....OASIS (Creation)	●

○ Silver (60,000 units)   ● Gold (100,000)   ★ Platinum (300,000)

Part of a monthly album chart

A pie chart is useful for showing the different sized divisions (slices) of one complete whole – the pie (e.g. types of hotel in a particular resort). Pie charts

can be confusing, however, if there are too many slices.

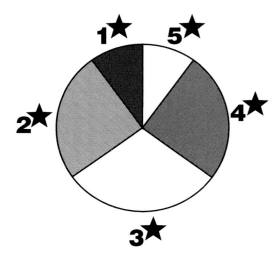

Types of hotel in a resort

The reader can see at a glance that there are few one star hotels in the resort, although further information would have to be added for the reader to know the actual number of hotels. You should use a protractor to divide pie charts accurately.

Bar charts (or column charts) tend to be most useful when you want to show selected examples of one factor (e.g. numbers of hotels in selected resorts). They have two axes (one vertical; one horizontal) and you can display as many bars as you wish. Bar charts work best when the differences are not so great as to make the vertical axis very long, or the shorter bars too small to distinguish.

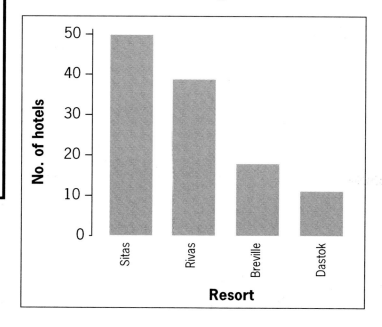

Flow charts

A flow chart shows the sequence of operations in a process and often uses arrows to show the direction of flow.

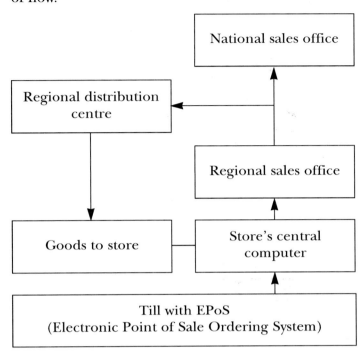

Pictograms

A pictogram uses pictures to represent information. A pictogram can be more eye-catching and fun to use than some other types of chart (see page 00).

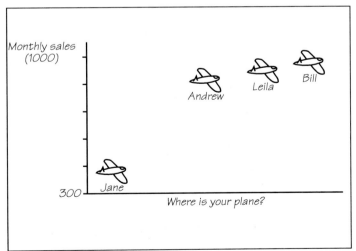

Tables

A table lists facts, numbers, etc., and is usually arranged in columns. The purpose of a table is to provide information to a reader in a form that is easy to read and useful. For example, the Table of Contents of a book enables the reader to go to a particular part without leafing through the entire book.

Here are two examples of tables:

Category	1	2	3	4
Mobility	Fully mobile/ Independent	Uses aids, e.g. zimmer, stick, occ. use of wheelchair	Needs wheelchair. Some use in hands and arms.	Completely immobile. Total care required.
Communication	Is able to see, hear well and speak.	Some difficulty seeing, hearing, speaking, but copes well.	Dysphasic or hard of hearing, or partially sighted.	Aphasic/total deafness, blind. Uses aids – letter/picture cards, speech console

Part of the McLoughlin scale – Mobility and Communication

The table below is a printout from a computer spreadsheet program, which automatically labels rows and columns with numbers and letters, for easy reference to each 'cell'. Spreadsheets are frequently used for business and accounting purposes.

	A	B	C	D	E	F	G
1		Jan	Feb	Mar	Apr	May	Jun
2							
3	Hardware sales	2300	1500	950	1700	2000	2200
4	Software sales	100	70	100	375	500	375
5	**Total sales**	2400	1570	1050	2075	2500	2575
6	Direct costs	800	650	700	700	675	725
7	Indirect costs	20	35	20	40	60	30
8	Overheads	350	70	100	200	100	200
9	**Total costs**	1170	755	820	940	835	955
10	**INCOME**	1230	815	230	1135	1665	1620

Photographs

A photograph is, literally, 'light writing' (photo = light; graph = writing). Photographs enable us to depict people, places and events that would be very time-consuming to portray in words. It is neither difficult nor expensive to produce a few photographs to illustrate what you wish to say or write, especially if you collaborate with others to share the costs.

Slides can be particularly effective to illustrate a presentation.

Video can also be used but it can be difficult and time-consuming to produce even a short video of suitable quality.

Overhead projector transparencies are easy to use so long as you bear in mind that the further people are from the screen, the larger images need to be; and that you should use few words or images because it is tedius to try and read a lot of material from a screen.

Maps

A map is a representation of the whole or some part of the physical world. It simplifies what it represents in order to help the user understand the image. (If the London Underground map showed the correct bends and turns of the tunnels, and the correct scaled distances, it would either be too huge to hold, or so complicated that no one would be able to follow it.)

So, if you are drawing a map, remember to keep it simple. Only put on major landmarks or other means by which users can orientate themselves; give a scale (is it 10 metres or 10 miles?). Remember, it only has to be fit for its purpose – not a work of art, or an accurate depiction of the world!

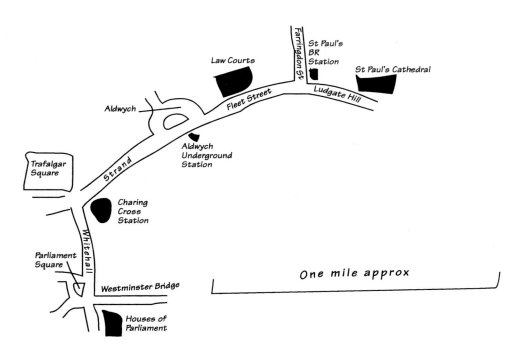

A simple hand-drawn map to show the route between St Paul's and the Houses of Parliament

Element 2.4 and 3.4: Read and respond to materials

Writing and reading are relatively recent human skills. Human beings have existed for millions of years, but the earliest examples of writing date back only a few thousand years. The need to keep records of business transactions seems to have been the spur to invent writing and its accompanying skill of reading.

The types of reading that are emphasised in Communication are linked to this earliest and continuing need to use language to record information and make it accessible in books, articles, reports, letters, memos and other formats.

Reading is carried out for a purpose, such as to obtain information, feedback, ideas, opinions and instructions. Having read material you then *use* it in some way, which is why the title of the element is *Read and <u>respond</u> to materials.*

Reading, like writing and all other skills, can be improved by practice. If you wish to play the guitar well, or cook to a high standard, you need to practice. Some people become frustrated by their lack of skill at reading and blame this on either themselves ('I'm stupid'), or on the writing ('It's boring'), when the truth is that they don't read often enough to build up a high level of skill. So, if you wish to read better, read often (whatever interests you – books, magazines, newspapers) and, like magic, your reading will improve!

Level

Whether a piece of writing is at LEVEL 2 or LEVEL 3 for the purpose of Communication depends on three factors:

- how complex the subject is – is it routine or non-routine; straightforward or complex?

- how complex the structure of the document is – is it an obvious and familiar structure; or complex and less familiar?

- the kind of help available to understand the document – is it provided for you; or do you have to seek out help yourself?

Thus, a letter or report on a subject that is familiar to you, when help is available from tutors and/or books, will be at LEVEL 2; whereas a book or lengthy report on a complex subject, when you have to seek out clarification on your own initiative, will be at LEVEL 3.

Remember that the level resides in the writing and not in the reader – someone used to reading scientific reports may read them with ease, yet the reports are still at LEVEL 3 or above; another person may find it very difficult to read a simple letter, and the letter will still only be at LEVEL 2.

UNDERSTANDING IMAGES

There is a well-known saying – 'There are lies, damned lies, and statistics'. Care needs to be taken when interpreting images, especially those that present statistics. Imagine a banner headline – CRIME FIGURE SOARS! – accompanied by this graph:

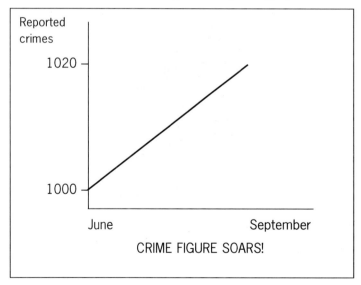

CRIME FIGURE SOARS!

However, if you look at the vertical scale, you will see that there are only 20 more crimes, from 1000, to 1020, which is not as dramatic as the headline suggests. Similarly, if the horizontal time scale were to be extended to show a 12-month, rather than a 3-month period, it would be seen that crime actually fell and has not reached its former level:

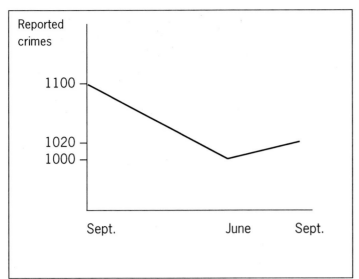

Thus, the choice of vertical and horizontal scales can affect the meaning of a graph very profoundly. When reading this sort of image it is necessary to pay close attention to the value of the scales to avoid being misled.

A general principle for interpreting images is *read the labels*. This applies not only to graphs and charts, but to many other images too. For instance, say you come across the following:

Unless you read the label, or have come across the image before, you may misinterpret it.

The label reads 'Risk of long hair being drawn into air inlet'.

Reading the labelling on diagrams is particularly important for electrical wiring diagrams, when a misreading can lead to death or serious injury.

If you do not understand an image, consult another person.

BEING SELECTIVE ABOUT WHAT YOU READ

There is so much information available today that no one can possibly read more than a tiny fraction of what has been written. You have to be selective – first

of all about which books, articles, etc. to read, and secondly, about how carefully you want to read what you select.

If you wish to research a particular topic there may be a range of ways of gathering information (e.g. questioning people or conducting experiments). A very effective way of gathering information is to read what other people have written about the topic. You may know someone who can give you advice about what to read or can lend you material, or you may need to use a library.

 STOP AND THINK
Do you use suitable techniques to select relevant information? Do you know how to use a library effectively?

Using a library

Libraries were opened shortly after the invention of writing. The first public library was opened at Athens in 330 BC. Public libraries and college libraries are treasure houses of information and ideas, and it is worth finding out how to use them efficiently. Browsing along the shelves can be an interesting way to spend some time, but if you wish to find information quickly, it is necessary to know how to use the library's classification system.

There are two main classification systems in current use: the Universal Decimal Classification (formerly the Dewey Decimal system), and the Library of Congress Classification. Every library has a catalogue to show readers which books and journals are available. A catalogue may be on cards, microfiche or a database. The most effective way to learn about the system in your library is to use it. Most librarians are happy to explain the system and help people find their way about – just ask.

Here is an example of a library search in a large library using an on-line database:

Step 1: Decide which topic you wish to find out about (the more specific you can be, the more likely it is that you will find what you need).

Let us assume the topic is language.

Step 2: The information on screen reads:

```
On-line catalogue main menu
Please type one of the following letters and
press RETURN
    T   for Title search
    A   for Author and name search
```

```
K   for searching Keywords within titles
S   for Subject search
C   for Class number search
```

You decide to type **K**, to search for the keyword 'language'. When you have typed in the keyword, the program informs you that:

There are 3030 references matching your enquiry

You could scroll through all 3030 titles, which would take a long time, or, the computer tells you, press **C** to continue the search. When you do this, the program offers you a number of alternatives, including:

1. Continue with another word to NARROW your search

You type in 'education', because you are interested in language in education. The program informs you that:

There are 941 references matching your enquiry

You decide to narrow the search even further by using another option:

4. Restrict your search by date of publication

You type in '1988' – to request titles of books about language in education published in 1988 or after. The program informs you that:

There are 210 references matching your enquiry

This is still too many, so you narrow the search still further by using option 1 (narrow your search with another word) and typing 'English'. The program informs you that:

There are 19 references matching your enquiry

You then scroll through the references and request more information about the second book on the list. The program informs you of the title, date of publication, author (in this case the Department for Education), publisher (in this case Her Majesty's Stationery Office), and classification number, in the Universal Decimal Classification, under which you will find the publication shelved:

English Language and Education, **1991**
Great Britain, Department for Education, London, HMSO
372.4/GRE

You may then go to the shelf where the 372 classification books are stored, take down the publication and dip into it to see whether it is worth borrowing.

This process need only take a few minutes once you are used to it. Imagine, instead, having to search a large library for a book on English language and education without the help of a catalogue – it may take you days.

Smaller libraries may not have an on-line catalogue system and you may have to search a card index. Some indexes are arranged alphabetically by author; others by subject; others by class number. Once again, the best way to familiarise yourself with a card index is to use it. The information that a card provides will be similar to that of an on-line system (i.e. title and date of publication; author and publisher; shelf number).

Imagine having to search a large library for a book on English Language without a Catalogue.

The Dewey classification system

In Britain the most common classification system for publications is called the Dewey system (now the Universal Decimal Classification). In this system, each subject is allocated a number as follows:

000 GENERAL WORKS

100 PHILOSOPHY

200 RELIGION

300 SOCIAL SCIENCES

400 LANGUAGE

500 PURE SCIENCES

600 TECHNOLOGY (APPLIED SCIENCES)

700 THE ARTS

800 LITERATURE

900 HISTORY, GEOGRAPHY, BIOGRAPHY

Within each broad classification, there are more detailed subject divisions. For example:

600 TECHNOLOGY (APPLIED SCIENCES)

  610 MEDICAL SCIENCE
  620 ENGINEERING
  630 AGRICULTURE, FOOD PRODUCTION
  640 HOME ECONOMICS, HOUSECRAFT
  650 BUSINESS AND BUSINESS METHODS
  660 CHEMICAL TECHNOLOGY
  670 PROCESSING TRADES
  680 CRAFT TRADES
  690 BUILDING

Within each of these classifications there are further, more precise, breakdowns – for example, 643.7 classifies books on do-it-yourself activities.

Journals

Journals are also classified using the Dewey system. For example, at J658 you will find management journals. If you wish to research a particular topic, it may be necessary to consult an indexing journal (which lists articles, by subject, in a number of journals) or an abstracting journal (which gives a summary – or 'abstract' – of articles in a number of journals) in order to find out which journals to read.

Floorplans

Each library has a floorplan to show which shelves hold which classifications. All you have to do is go to the appropriate shelf to find the publication you want.

Using CD-ROM

Compact Disc Read-Only Memory (CD-ROM) is a computer disc that can store vast amounts of information and make it readily accessible to readers. Large reference works (such as dictionaries, encyclopedias, technical manuals), databases of articles from books, newspapers and journals, and directories (such as information about companies and marketing) are all available on CD-ROM.

CD-ROM enables users to print out information, and to retrieve information and store it on a floppy disk.

Specialist databases

In addition to general databases, some libraries may have access to specialist databases, such as Datastream, which gives access to company accounts and share information.

Interlibrary loans

If you can't find the information you need in your library, it is possible (for a small charge) to request that the book or article be transferred from another library, through the interlibrary loan system. The librarians will have details.

Using reference books

All libraries stock a range of reference books, containing a wealth of useful information. They cannot usually be borrowed, but are intended to be dipped into for information. Consult a:

Dictionary – for definitions of words, examples of their use, pronunciation. When you consult a dictionary you will often be given a number of possible meanings of a word. The appropriate meaning depends on the context of use, i.e. you need to consider which meaning is appropriate in a particular sentence.

Subject dictionary – for definitions of words relevant to a particular subject (e.g. Business, Electronics, Environment, Information Technology)

Thesaurus – for alternative words from which to choose

Encyclopedia – for brief information about any subject

There are many other reference works, e.g. to specific subjects; local businesses; government statistics; countries of the world.

The use of suitable reference books can be a quick and efficient way of gathering information, and can prepare the ground for more detailed study of other books on a subject.

It is sometimes necessary to consult more than one reference to clarify the meaning of a word or phrase. For example, if you are going abroad and a leaflet recommends that you be vaccinated against yellow fever and you wish to know a little about the disease, a dictionary may tell you very little (e.g. yellow fever = tropical viral disease with fever and jaundice). If you want to know a little more it would be a good idea to consult a general encyclopedia, where you will discover that yellow fever is carried by the Stegomyia mosquito found in South and Central America and African ports. If you want a lot more information it will be necessary to consult a medical dictionary or other medical text.

Using telephone directories

Like other books, most telephone directories have a Table of Contents at the front, and some have a Classification Index at the back to help readers use the directory efficiently. For example, if you wish to discover which shops in your area can sell you a CD-ROM system, it may be necessary to consult the Classification Index for suitable sections of the *Yellow Pages* (e.g. Computers: peripherals, or alternatively, Audio Dealers: TV, Video & Radio Shops).

Mining a Book.

Mining books for information

Once you have found books or any other written materials that seem likely to contain the information you seek, you may be tempted to read them from beginning to end. This is time-consuming and often unnecessary. Reading is not a one-gear activity. Novels are usually read from cover to cover and fairly slowly – sometimes we don't want them to end. Poetry is sometimes read even more intensively, and the reader may ponder meaning, word use and rhythm. For the purposes of most communication, however, you need only extract or 'mine' the information and ideas that you seek. To do this it helps to have a clear question or focus in mind when reading.

STOP AND THINK
How many reading gears do you have? Can you find the information you seek quickly? Do you need more practice in scanning and skimming?

Scanning, skimming, studying

The parts of a book that are likely to give you a quick overview of what it contains are the *Contents* page, the *Index* (at the back of the book) and, if the book has them, the *Summaries* (at the beginning or end of chapters).

All of these will give you clues about where to dip into the book for suitable material. Often the beginnings of chapters contain strong clues to what follows; and the ends of chapters often summarise what has gone before.

You can also scan through whole books, or whole chapters, allowing your eyes to take in large blocks of print, searching for the clues to relevant material. Then you can skim a number of pages, reading superficially, extracting only the main points. It is not necessary to always read forwards in a book or article – sometimes you will need to move backwards and forwards until you find what you are looking for.

Once you have found particular passages that are of interest to you, you may slow down to study the material, by reading it at a slower pace and perhaps making a few notes (see *Making notes*). If when reading you come across a term that you don't understand, you will find that the context often provides clues to meaning. Don't try to read text very closely, or stumble over individual words and sentences. Read quite quickly, ignore some of the detail and see how the main argument shapes. In this way, many words or phrases that may at first seem difficult will become clearer.

When you come across an unfamiliar word, the Index may show where else in the book the word is used and, by looking at its use several times, it is possible to work out the meaning, without needing to seek further clarification.

In this way you can mine many books in a short time, discarding books that seem irrelevant to your needs, and quickly extracting the information you need from others.

A quick way to remember how to mine books for information is **SQ3R**:

Scan the materials to get an overview; have some

Questions in mind you want answered; **R**ead the materials at whatever pace is appropriate (skim or study); **R**ecall what you have read from time to time by writing a brief summary; finally, **R**eview your summary.

Understanding the subject

Often, when you read through written material for information or ideas you will already have some knowledge about the subject and what you are looking for. Identifying the main points or following the line of argument may, therefore, be relatively easy. However, sometimes you will need to read material with which you are not familiar; or to read material that is so complex that you will need help to understand it.

Some clarification of the main points can be gained from reading with care, making some notes, and consulting a dictionary or other reference work when necessary. In addition, you will find that it is sometimes necessary to consult other people. Some people find it difficult to ask another person for help. They feel it is like an admission of weakness. It is not. As the great scientist, Isaac Newton said, 'If I have seen far, it is by standing on the shoulders of giants'. Today you may seek help from another person, tomorrow it may be you who is asked for help.

Another means of clarification is to simply leave the apparent difficulty for a while. Do something else, and return to it afresh at another time. Very often the difficulty will have vanished – it was only tiredness or over-familiarity that led to you not seeing the obvious.

Reading, like speaking, listening and writing is not carried out by the mind alone. Our hearts and souls are also involved. For example, if someone writes you a letter of complaint that is less than tactfully expressed, you may feel a sense of hurt pride – 'How dare they' – that gets in the way of taking in the main points the letter makes. It is impossible to switch off our feelings completely when reading, but it is possible to be aware that our feelings can sometimes get in the way of understanding. If you find you are reacting emotionally to something, a cooling-off period before you reply is often a good idea.

 STOP AND THINK
Do you sometimes react too hastily when it would be wiser to consider your reply?

Making notes

Whether you are reading, preparing to speak or write, or recording what has been agreed, you will often need to make notes.

Here are some hints for making useful notes:

Making notes and summaries

Making notes from written materials

In order to summarise the information from books and other written materials, it is helpful to use index cards that can be stored in a file box. Summaries are usually written in your own words but, sometimes, for accuracy or impact, it is necessary to quote from the original material. If you wish to quote from a book or article, or list it in a bibliography or reference section, be sure to record the author, year of publication, title and publisher at the top of the first card like this:

Robinson, Peter (1995) Information
Technology for Service GNVQs, Collins
Educational.

Avoid the temptation to make lengthy summary notes. It is time-consuming and the result may be a dense mass of writing more difficult to read than the book itself. Summarising information involves identifying the main points from the extracted material and presenting them in a concise form, either orally or in writing.

It is very inconsiderate to mark a book that other people will use. However, if you feel you must write in the book itself, write in light pencil in the margin

Avoid the temptation to make lengthy notes.

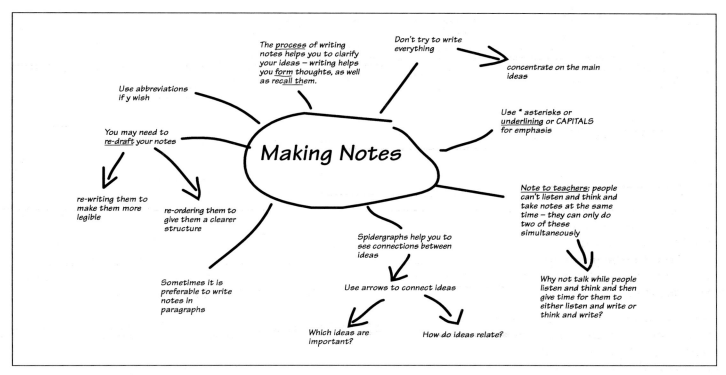

The process of writing notes helps you to clarify your ideas – writing helps you <u>form</u> thoughts, as well as <u>recall</u> them.

Don't try to write everything → concentrate on the main ideas

Use abbreviations if y wish

Use * asterisks or <u>underlining</u> or CAPITALS for emphasis

You may need to <u>re-draft</u> your notes

Making Notes

<u>Note to teachers</u>: people can't listen and think and take notes at the same time – they can only do two of these simultaneously

re-writing them to make them more legible

re-ordering them to give them a clearer structure

Spidergraphs help you to see connections between ideas

Why not talk while people listen and think and then give time for them to either listen and write or think and write?

Sometimes it is preferable to write notes in paragraphs

Use arrows to connect ideas

Which ideas are important?

How do ideas relate?

by anything you think may be noteworthy. Go back from time to time (e.g. after a chapter) to look again at what you have marked. Sometimes it will no longer seem worth noting, perhaps because there is a better statement later. If it is noteworthy make brief notes, using abbreviations if you wish (usg abbrev if y wsh).

Remember to record accurately any words you might want to quote, and make a page reference.

If you don't own the book, rub out the light pencil. <u>Never</u> mark a book in ink. This will ruin it for future use.

STOP AND THINK
How efficiently do you make notes? Do you read material without making sufficient notes? Are you a dreaded book-marker who ruins books for other readers?

Judging the relevance of materials

Book and articles are written by human beings, all of whom are fallible. People express opinions and ideas which may or may not be correct, and they interpret facts according to particular standpoints of culture, circumstance and politics. When researching a topic it is sometimes necessary to read a range of materials in order to obtain a balanced view. This is especially the case when reading newspapers, most of which tend towards one political party.

The writers of books, articles and newspapers may put a bias on information they present by, for example:

- giving excessive prominence to facts and opinions that they agree with;

- ignoring facts and opinions that they disagree with;

- including facts and opinions that they disagree with but, consciously or subconsciously, misrepresenting them, either directly or by the use of biased language. One paper's 'peace initiative' may be another's 'propaganda ploy'; one political party may 'win' seats while another 'grabs' them; the same people may be called 'freedom fighters' or 'terrorists'. People who hold different views to the paper's may simply be dismissed as 'loonies', without any attempt to present their ideas;

- including facts and opinions that they disagree with but giving them little prominence.

- using photographs that have been trimmed or angled to show only what the paper wishes. For example, a few days before a general election, one paper showed a Labour leader addressing a public meeting attended apparently by only children. The rest of the audience had been cut out of the photograph.

(Examples taken from Keane, 1991)

	Position in newspaper	Total number of words (approx)	Direct quotes from Powntree report (no. of words)	Explanatory images
Daily Mail (tends to support Conservative)	p. 15	700	160	0
Daily Mirror (tends to support Labour)	pp. 6 and 7	1000	2⁻9	2
The Guardian (tends to support Labour/Liberal)	p. 1 and p. 15	1400	236	3
The Sun (tends to support Conservative)	p. 6	80 (but not directly about Rowntree report)	0	0

Consider the coverage on 10 February 1995 by four national newspapers of a major report by the Rowntree Trust on Income and Wealth in Britain (see table above).

STOP AND THINK
Do you read a newspaper? Which political party does it tend to support and how does this affect its coverage of news?

When researching a topic it is sometimes preferable to go to primary sources (i.e. to the actual report or research, rather than to second-hand accounts).

However, this is often impracticable – the primary sources may not be available; you may not have time to consult them; they may be written for a specialist audience and not be understandable by other readers.

In practice, we have to rely on the accuracy and honesty of much that we read, but we should avoid thinking of printed text as embodying sacred wisdom – it rarely does, but instead presents the opinions and interpretations of fallible human beings. To compensate for this, it is wise to consult a range of materials in order to judge their relevance.